Tempus
Two in One Series

SUNDERLAND
AFC

Tempus
Two in One Series

SUNDERLAND
AFC

Compiled by
Alan Brett and George Hoare

TEMPUS

THE
Archive Photographs
SERIES

SUNDERLAND AFC
1879-1973

Compiled by
Alan Brett and George Hoare

TEMPUS

This edition first published 2001
Copyright © Alan Brett and George Hoare, 2001

Tempus Publishing Limited
The Mill, Brimscombe Port,
Stroud, Gloucestershire, GL5 2QG

ISBN 0 7524 2216 2

Typesetting and origination by
Tempus Publishing Limited
Printed in Great Britain by
Midway Clark Printing, Wiltshire

Originally produced as two books:

Sunderland AFC 1879-1973
First published 1996
Copyright © Alan Brett and George Hoare, 1996
ISBN 0 7524 0716 3

Roker Park Voices
First published 1997
Copyright © Alan Brett and Andrew Clark, 1997
ISBN 0 7524 1063 6

Contents

Blackpool goalkeeper George Farm in action at Roker Park. In the late 1940s and early '50s th
star-studded Blackpool side containing the likes of Stanley Matthews and Stan Mortensen we
one of the biggest attractions in the game. On 12 April 1948 the Seasiders drew a record Leagu
attendance to Roker Park of 61,084. New figures were again set by Blackpool's visit th
following season with 64,889 packing the ground.

Acknowledgements

The Authors would like to thank the following individuals and organisations for their help
with this publication.

Stuart Bell, Thomas Carney, Keith Charlton, Phil Curtis, *Daily Express*, David Dodds,
Evening Standard, *Football Echo*, George Forster, Peter Gibson, Phil Hall, Harry Langton,
London Illustrated News, Monkwearmouth Library, Alex Murray,
Newcastle Chronicle & Journal, *Northeast Press*, Pat O'Brien, *Shields Gazette*, *Sunday Pictorial*,
Sunderland Central Library, *Sunderland Echo*, Sunderland Supporters' Association,
Weekly Courier, *Weekly Illustrated*.

Special thanks to Andrew Clark, North East Editor of Chalford Publishing.

Bibliography

Raich Carter, *Footballer's Progress*, Sporting Handbooks 1950
Charles Buchan, *A Lifetime in Football*, Phoenix House 1950
Alfred Gibson & William Pickford, *Association Football & The Men Who Made It*, Caxton 190
Simon Inglis, *Football Grounds of England and Wales*, Collins 1983
Simon Inglis, *Soccer in the Dock*, Collins 1985
Len Shackleton, *Clown Prince of Soccer*, Nicholas Kaye 1955
Alan Brett & Andrew Clark, *Sunderland Annuals 1990 – 1996*, Black Cat Publications
Alan Brett & Andrew Clark, *Newcastle United v Sunderland*, Black Cat Publications 1995

Introduction

his unique collection of photographs and memorabilia was amassed over a half a century and
ustrates Sunderland's remarkable history. Formed in 1879 by a group of local schoolteachers,
ter opening its doors to outsiders the club never looked back. Even before entering the
ootball League, Sunderland already had an outstanding side and were known as the 'Team of
ll the Talents.'

Having first played on the Blue House Field the club made several moves in the early years.
hese included Groves Field, Horatio Street and Abbs Field before settling at Newcastle Road.
om September 1890 Sunderland lost only one home game in the next six years. With Scottish
ars like Ted Doig, Johnny Campbell and Hugh Wilson Sunderland won three championship
uring this period.

After moving to Roker Park in 1898 success continued and a fourth championship was won.
his period before the First World War was another golden era for the club. Its most famous
ctory came on 5 December 1908 when deadly rivals Newcastle United were thrashed 9-1 at St
mes' Park. In the 1912-13 season the League and Cup 'Double' was almost achieved but a 1-0
:feat by Aston Villa before a 120,000 crowd at Crystal Palace ended this dream.

Sunderland's FA Cup jinx was to last almost a quarter of century until Hendon-born Raich
arter became the first Roker skipper to lift the famous trophy. This outstanding side had
aimed Sunderland's sixth championship trophy the previous season. At this time Sunderland
ew record crowds around the country and this continued after the Second World War when
iey were named the 'Bank of England Club'. Their big spending in the transfer market failed
> bring further honours to Roker Park. The closest they came to a further League title came in
ie 1949-50 season. A freak defeat at the hands of bottom of the table Manchester City at
oker Park cost Sunderland the championship. During this season the aggregate attendance
ipped the one million mark for the first time.

Sunderland's proud record of only having played in the top division came to an end in 1958
hen the club suffered its first ever relegation. After coming heartbreakingly close to
:omotion on a number of occasions a return to the top flight was finally achieved under the
adership of 'Player of the Century' Charlie Hurley.

By the end of the decade Sunderland were again relegated and the club's fortunes were at one
' the lowest points in its history. The appointment of Bob Stokoe was to inspire a revival. The
iry tale success at Wembley brought Sunderland back to the centre of the world stage.

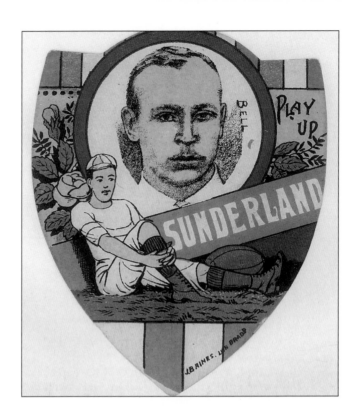

Roll of Honour

Football League Champions

1891-92
1892-93
1894-95
1901-02
1912-13
1935-36

FA Cup Winners

1937
1973

One

Early Days
1879-1900

Schooldays to Glory Days

Hendon Board School can stake a claim as the birthplace of football in Sunderland. When Scotsman James Allan took up a teaching post at the school he introduced the Association code to Wearside, where rugby had previously flourished. A meeting at the British Day School, Norfolk Street in October 1879 led to the formation of Sunderland and District Teachers' Association Football Club. For the first three seasons they played at the nearby Blue House Field before moving to Groves Field at Ashbrooke.

Former Hendon Board schoolboy Raich Carter after becoming the first Sunderland captain to receive the FA Cup. After being one of the top clubs in the country for half a century the Cup had always eluded Sunderland teams. After the Wembley triumph in 1937 Sunderland had to wait until 1973 before they won their next trophy. However, during this lean spell Sunderland were at times still the most famous club in England.

Sunderland line-up in 1884 kitted out in blue shirts and knickerbockers. Back row: Kirtley, McMillan, Lumsden, Singleton, Murdoch. Middle row: McDonald, J. Allan, Hall, Grayston, J.M. Allan. Front row: Leslie, Wade, Innes. During the 1883-84 season Sunderland played at the 'Clay Dolly Field' off Horatio Street at Roker. There were no dressing rooms so the players changed at The Wolseley public house nearby. At the end of the season Sunderland reached the Final of the Durham Challenge Cup. On 5 April 1884 they met Darlington at the old Cricket Ground, Newcastle Road. Before a crowd of between one and two thousand people Sunderland started playing 'up the hill'. At the end of an exciting contest Sunderland ran out 4-3 winners having trailed for most of the game. Darlington lodged a protest on the grounds their players had been intimidated by some of the home supporters. The referee also said he was threatened by three Sunderland players. This resulted in the Final being replayed at Birtley on 10 May. Cheap trips were organised by the North-Eastern Railway Company and many supporters took the opportunity to travel to see the match. Goals from Joyce and McDonald gave Sunderland a 2-0 victory to win the Cup 'again'. The following season the club moved to a new ground at Abbs Field in Fulwell. Sunderland reached the Durham Challenge Cup Final again and their opponents were again Darlington. The Quakers won the match 3-0 at Feethams and this time it was Sunderland's turn to protest at intimidation. The objections were dismissed and Darlington held on to the trophy.

Sunderland-born Charles W. Alcock was one of the most important figures in the history of football. He was appointed Secretary of the Football Association in 1870 at the age of 28. Within two years two momentous milestones had been achieved. In 1871 what was to become the most famous competition in the world was started – the FA Challenge Cup. The following year the first official international match took place – England played Scotland at Glasgow. A Sunderland man had laid the football foundations for the rest of the world to follow.

Before Sunderland entered the Football League they had already played in half a dozen FA Cup competitions. Sunderland's first tie was on 8 November 1884 at Redcar (the preliminary rounds were regional). Redcar won 3-1 and the following season Sunderland went out to the same club 3-0. Controversy was soon to dog Sunderland in the competition. They were disqualified in 1887-88 for playing three ineligible players against Middlesbrough. The following season they withdrew from the Cup rather than play Sunderland Albion. By the time Sunderland finally won the FA Cup they received a different trophy. The original cup was stolen when on display in a Birmingham shop window in 1895.

y 1885-86 Sunderland were playing in halved shirts which gave way to the famous red and hite stripes by 1888. Back row: Wallace (secretary), Hunter, Turner (boot cleaner), Kirtley, lliott, Todd (committee). Middle row: Marshall, Dale, Reed (chairman), McMillan. Front w: Erskine, Smith, Hornsby, Jobes, Smart. Sunderland were on the move again in April 1886 quiring a field at Newcastle Road which they developed into a top class venue. This was an nportant period in Sunderland's history as men like shipbuilders Robert Thompson and James 1arr and coal-owner Samuel Tyzack joined the club. The appointment of Tom Watson as cretary/manager was to signal the beginning of a golden age on Wearside built on the back of nported Scottish talent. At this time poaching players north of the border was a hazardous ccupation with those caught receiving a severe beating. On one occasion Tyzack borrowed the erical garb of Reverend McGonagle to avoid detection. The reward for this subterfuge was the sembling of one of the greatest sides in the land. Players brought south included: Johnny ampbell, Johnny Harvey and David Hannah from Renton; Tom Porteous and John Smith om Kilmarnock; Jack Scott from Coatbridge Albion Rovers and John Auld from Third anark. After a 7-2 victory over Aston Villa in a friendly in 1889, the Football League founder 'illiam McGregor was moved to say, 'Sunderland had a talented man in every position'. Thus ven before Sunderland entered the League they had earned the title the 'Team of All the alents'.

Sunderland Albion. Back row: Allison (committee), Campbell (trainer), McDermid, Angu
McFarlene, Coates (hon. secretary), Glass (vice-chairman). Middle row: Hannah, Whit
McNichol, Stewart, Brand. Front row: Smith, Weir, Kinnaird. Albion had been founded b
James Allan and other disgruntled Sunderland members in March 1888. The new clu
attracted many of Sunderland's Scottish players which helped them to become quickl
established on the field.

A card promoting the new club. In the 1888-89 season Sunderland were drawn against Sunderland Albion in both the FA Cup and Durham Cup. Rather than help swell their rivals' coffers Sunderland scratched from both competitions. The public on Wearside insisted on a showdown so the clubs agreed to meet in a friendly on 1 December 1888. A crowd of over 10,000 at Newcastle Road produced the first three figure gate receipts in the history of football in the region. The sum of £151 left each club with over £70 profit once expenses had been paid. Sunderland won the 'derby' clash 2-0.

underland team of 1889-90, the last season before entering the League. Back row: Porteous, irtley, Watson (secretary), Oliver. Middle row: Harvey, Stevenson, Auld, Gibson, Scott. ront row: Smith, Campbell, Hannah. Eight of the players appeared in Sunderland's first ever eague match on 13 September 1890. Scotsmen Harvey, Stevenson and Smith were replaced y fellow countrymen Wilson, Spence and Millar for the game.

souvenir card dating from around 1890. underland were one of the clubs featured in e series, with strip accuracy not always a ajor consideration. In the 1890-91 season underland were admitted to the Football eague at the expense of Stoke City. At this me footballers had to supplement their 25 illings a week wages from football (10 illings close season) with outside work. underland players found work at the North ands or Manor Quay shipyards, Dickinson's ngine Works and Wearmouth Foundry in onk Street.

After playing in Sunderland's first ever League game Hugh Wilson went on to help the club to championship triumphs in 1891-92, 1892-93 and 1894-95. The long distances the Scottish international achieved with his one-handed throws caused havoc in opponents' goalmouths. This led to a change in the law and the introduction of the two-handed throw.

Like many of his fellow Scots Jimmy Millar was lured south by good wages, signing-on fees, match bonuses and some were even set up in business. After signing from Annbank in 1890 he was a regular in the Sunderland team that won three championships. In 1896 Millar joined Glasgow Rangers but returned to play an important part in the club's fourth title in 1901-02.

The famous Thomas Hemy painting of a Sunderland-Aston Villa game at Newcastle Road in 1895. The first match at the ground had been played on 3 April 1886 with Darlington providing the opposition. The club built up the stadium until it was the largest in the North East and in 1891 it staged the England-Wales match. After a dozen seasons at Newcastle Road the move was made to Roker Park.

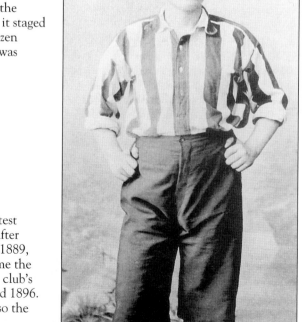

Johnny Campbell was one of the greatest goalscorers of early League football. After signing from Scottish club Renton in 1889, the 5ft 7in, 13st, centre forward became the terror of English defences. He was the club's top scorer five times between 1890 and 1896. On three of these occasions he was also the top marksman in the entire League.

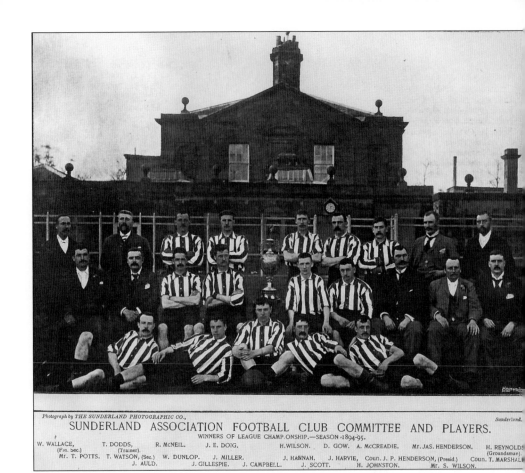

Photograph by THE SUNDERLAND PHOTOGRAPHIC CO.,

Sunderland.

SUNDERLAND ASSOCIATION FOOTBALL CLUB COMMITTEE AND PLAYERS.

WINNERS OF LEAGUE CHAMP.ONSHIP.—SEASON ·1894-95.

W. WALLACE,   T. DODDS,   R. McNEIL.   J. E. DOIG.   H.WILSON.   D. GOW.   A. McCREADIE.   Mr. JAS. HENDERSON.   H. REYNOLDS
(Fin. Sec.)   (Trainer).   (Groundsman).
Mr. T. POTTS,   T. WATSON, (Sec.)   W. DUNLOP.   J. MILLER.   J. HANNAH,   J. HARVIE,   Coun. J. P. HENDERSON, (Presid.)   Coun. T. MARSHALL
J. AULD.   J. GILLESPIE.   J. CAMPBELL.   J. SCOTT.   H. JOHNSTON.   Mr. S. WILSON.

Sunderland's third championship-winning side in four years. The team, with Scotsmen still to the forefront, also had a good Cup run. In the First Round Fairfield were swept away by a record 11-1 scoreline. Victories over Preston North End and Bolton Wanderers brought a semi-final meeting with Aston Villa. The Birmingham club were again to prove Sunderland's bogey team, eventually going on to win the Cup.

Hailed as one of the finest left backs of his generation Jimmy Watson was to play over 200 League games for Sunderland between 1900 and 1907. He made four appearances for Scotland whilst at Roker and in one of these, against England, he played alongside team-mates Ted Doig and Andy McCombie. In April 1907 Watson moved to Middlesbrough, helping the Teessiders to the best defensive record in the League in his first season. His displays were also recognised at international level after an interval of four years. He was recalled for the match against Ireland in 1909 at the age of 31 and weighing 13½st. He was selected for the last time in the next game against England.

Watson

"UMPIRE" FAVOURITES.

THE UMPIRE:
The Best
Weekly Paper
for
General News
and Sport.

Reproduced from
THE UMPIRE
of Jan. 24 1904.

G.E.Ton

ANDREW McCOMBIE (SUNDERLAND).

Scotland international Andy McCombie was one of the best full backs in the game at the turn of the century. After six seasons with Sunderland he left in controversial circumstances. A dispute arose as to whether money given to McCombie by the club to start up a business was a gift or a loan. A court case and an FA inquiry followed and the club was fined and directors suspended. McCombie was transferred to neighbours Newcastle for a record £700 fee. At Gallowgate he added a further two caps to his collection before retiring in 1910. He then joined United's coaching staff where he remained for the next forty years.

After making his debut in Sunderland's third ever game in the League Ted Doig went on to become a legend on Wearside. Already a Scottish international with Arbroath he won a further three caps in a Roker career spanning fourteen seasons. His goalkeeping talents were still in demand in 1904 at the age of thirty-seven. Former Sunderland secretary Tom Watson took him to Liverpool. He made an immediate impact helping Liverpool to the Second Division title in his first season.

A postcard of a derby match at St James' Park. The scene depicted owes a fair amount to artistic licence. Sunderland's first League visit to Newcastle took place on 22 April 1899. A goal from McLatchie gave Sunderland a 1-0 victory.

Two

The New Century
1900-15

Another title
then almost the 'Double'

Jackson "Left Half"

After winning an FA Amateur Cup medal with Middlesbrough Richard 'Dicky' Jackson joined Sunderland in the 1898 close season. Once he got established in professional football he went on to become Sunderland captain. His loyalty to the club was rewarded with a benefit on New Year's Eve 1904 which he shared with Billy Hogg.

The Sheffield Wednesday programme for Sunderland's League visit in the 1900-01 season. At the time Sunderland were top of the table with only two games left but a 1-0 defeat against Wednesday allowed Liverpool to snatch the title.

he team photograph from the programme celebrating the 1901-02 title. Although the cup in 1e picture is not the championship trophy. The team had got over the disappointment of being 1nners-up to Liverpool the previous season to bounce back as champions.

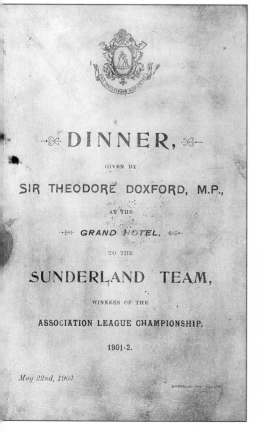

-✂- DINNER, -✂-

GIVEN BY

SIR THEODORE DOXFORD, M.P.,

AT THE

-≡- GRAND HOTEL, -≡-

TO THE

SUNDERLAND TEAM,

WINNERS OF THE

ASSOCIATION LEAGUE CHAMPIONSHIP,

1901-2.

May 22nd, 1902

SUNDERLAND PORT CO. LTD.

Sunderland MP Sir W. Theodore Doxford honoured a promise that if the club won the championship he would treat the players and officials to a celebration dinner. The Grand Hotel in Bridge Street hosted the event on 22 May 1902. In a speech, club chairman J.P. Henderson recalled how Sunderland had to travel something like 6,000 miles to achieve their triumph. On one occasion the team were stranded in York for several hours – 'that was fun in the depth of winter.'

Barrie
Centre Half

An unusual shot of Sunderland's squad in the 1902-03 season. It shows how Roker Park looked at the turn of the century. Although the capacity was a vast improvement on Newcastle Road, the low terracing and old grandstand could still not hold the massive crowds it was to later accommodate. The largest pre-First World War crowd was for West Bromwich Albion FA Cup visit on 24 February 1912. The official attendance was 43,383 but many more climbed over the railings to get in. The second half had to be delayed because the crowd spilled onto the pitch.

After signing from Glasgow Park Head in the 1902 close season Alex Barrie found it difficult to break into the reigning champions side. He made only three appearances in the 1902-03 season but did score in the 4-2 win over Grimsby Town. After another four seasons in and out of the team he returned to Glasgow, this time to the mighty Rangers.

mmy Gemmell was joint leading scorer in
e 1901-02 championship-winning side
ith 10 goals. Sunderland spotted his
tential when he played against them in a
iendly for Clyde. He was only 19 years old
hen he signed in November 1900 but he
ade rapid progress and was soon in the first
am. In two spells with the club the skilful
side left made over 200 League
pearances.

Sunderland-born Alf Common holds a unique
place in English football, having been the first
£500 transfer and the first four figure transfer. In
1900 he joined his hometown club but within
eighteen months was on the move to Sheffield
United for a fee of £325. Whilst with United the
striker won two England caps and scored in an
FA Cup Final. In 1904 he returned to Roker for
£520. Eight months later Sunderland received
£1,000 from Middlesbrough for Common's
services.

A move from Willington Athletic to Sunderland in 1899 was to signal the start of a great career for Billy Hogg. A regular rather than prolific goalscorer, his talents were recognised at international level early on. He made his England debut against Wales in March 1902 when aged twenty-two.

Woolwich Arsenal V. Sunderland at Plumstead 21·10·05.

A rare early action photograph of a League match between Woolwich Arsenal and Sunderland on 21 October 1905. The Londoners ran out 2-0 winners at the Manor Ground in Plumstead. Eight years after the game the Gunners made the controversial decision to move lock, stock and barrel across the river to their present home in North London.

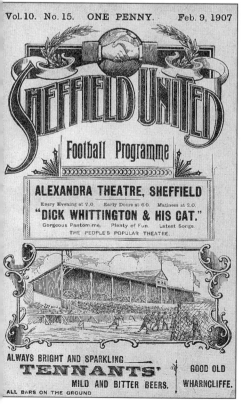

Vol. 10. No. 15.   ONE PENNY.   Feb. 9, 1907

SHEFFIELD UNITED
Football Programme

ALEXANDRA THEATRE, SHEFFIELD
Every Evening at 7.0.   Early Doors at 6.0.   Matinees at 2.0.
"DICK WHITTINGTON & HIS CAT."
Gorgeous Pantomime.   Plenty of Fun.   Latest Songs.
THE PEOPLE'S POPULAR THEATRE.

ALWAYS BRIGHT AND SPARKLING
TENNANTS'
MILD AND BITTER BEERS.
ALL BARS ON THE GROUND
GOOD OLD
WHARNCLIFFE.

Sheffield United's programme for the League game against Sunderland at Bramall Lane on 9 February 1907. Goals from McIntosh and Huggins could not prevent a 3-2 United victory. Having won at Roker earlier in the season the Blades thus completed the double over Sunderland.

27

Scenes from the FA Cup tie between Sunderland and Sheffield Wednesday on 23 February 1907. Before advances in printing technology allowed photographs of matches to appear in newspapers, sketches of the action were reproduced. A crowd of around 30,000 including over 700 from Wearside, witnessed a 0-0 draw. A few days later Wednesday snatched a 1-0 win in the replay at Roker. In 1914 Owlerton was renamed Hillsborough but the club are still known as the Owls.

…ly Agnew holds a special place in …orth East football as he was the first man … play for the 'Big Three' clubs. After …ning Newcastle from Kilmarnock in …'02 he remained at St James' for two …asons before joining Middlesbrough. …e then returned to Kilmarnock where he …n three caps. In May 1908 he made his …storic move to Roker Park.

SEASON 1908-9.

Copyright Photograph by W. A. Culshaw, 119 High St. West, Sunderland.

SUNDERLAND ASSOCIATION FOOTBALL CLUB,

ROKER PARK.

League Champions : 1891-2, 1892—3, 1894-5, 1901-2.

A postcard for the 1908-09 season showing the players, the old stand at Roker Park and the Black Cat. Sunderland were to finish the campaign in third place in the League. The most notable performance by far was the record 9-1 win at Newcastle. The scoreline stunned the football world. The *Daily Express* reported, 'But for sheer amazement we have known nothing like the result at Newcastle for years... the result was due absolutely to the remarkable form of Sunderland. Surely this is the greatest performance ever known in football.'

WILLIAM HOGG,
SUNDERLAND A.F.C.

A solitary Billy Hogg goal was all that Sunderland had to show going into the half time interval against Newcastle United at St James' Park on 5 December 1908. When he and his team-mates walked off at full time he had completed his hat-trick and Sunderland had achieved an amazing victory.

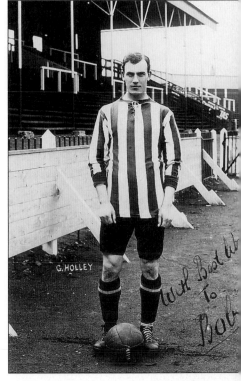

G. HOLLEY

George Holley was the first of Sunderland's two hat-trick men to complete the feat. The Seaham-born inside forward scored over 150 League and Cup goals for Sunderland. Four months after the Newcastle game he won the first of ten England caps (8 goals).

gland winger Arthur Bridgett found the net
ice in the 9-1 victory. For Bridgett some things
ne before football: he was involved with the
otherhood Movement and was a much sought
er preacher. He refused to play on Good
day or Christmas Day because of religious
nvictions. Fortunately for Sunderland the
James' Massacre' fell on an 'ordinary'
turday.

County Durham-born Jackie Mordue joined
Sunderland from Arsenal in the 1908 close
season. After barely a dozen League games
he faced his first Tyne-Wear derby. He was
to prove ready for the occasion: scoring
Sunderland's eighth goal in the 73rd minute
of the game. A few minutes later Hogg
completed the scoring and Sunderland eased
up for the last quarter of an hour of the
game.

The only member of the forward line to fail to score in the Newcastle rout was England international Arthur Brown. Before joining the club from Sheffield United the centre forward had become one of the youngest players ever to represent his country. He was still only eighteen when he played against Wales in February 1904. His precocious talent had earned him the nickname 'Boy' Brown. It was not only his England credentials that brought Brown to Sunderland's attention. In October 1907 he scored four goals against Sunderland in a League game at Bramall Lane.

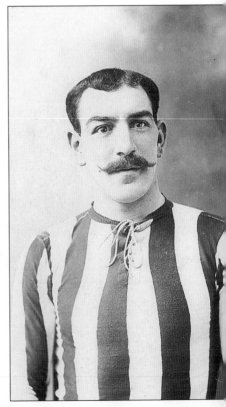

The imposing figure of Sunderland and Scotland captain Charlie Thomson. He was first capped with Hearts in 1904 and he continued as first choice centre half after his transfer to Sunderland in 1908. To secure his services Sunderland had to pay £700. At the time there was a transfer limit of £350 and the difference was made up by a make-weight player. His total of 21 caps was impressive in an age when internationals were limited to the Home Countries – three games a year.

rry Martin made his debut for Sunderland Good Friday 1912 and scored in the 2-1 eat at Liverpool. Arthur Bridgett's refusal play on religious grounds had left the door en for Martin's first appearance. The future gland international never looked back ile Bridgett never played for Sunderland in. The following month Bridgett was nsferred to South Shields.

H. MARTIN

Carluke-born Tommy Tait might have thought international honours had passed him by during his fifth season at Roker. But at the age of thirty-one Scotland called him up for the international against Wales in March 1911. Although he never played for his country again the Sunderland wing half had achieved every footballer's dream.

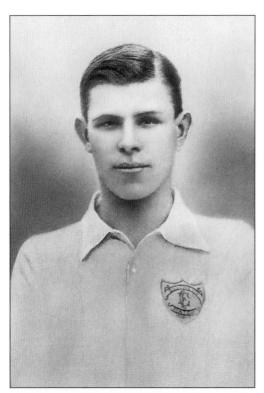

In March 1911 Charlie Buchan was transferred from Southern League Leyton Sunderland. On signing manager Bob Kyl told him: 'Son, it's very cold up north, so advise you to get an outfit of thick winter clothes. You'll need them.' He took his advice and bought an outfit of warm cloth and was grateful he did: it was snowing when he arrived on Wearside and it did no stop for four days.

The Sunderland squad for the 1912-13 campaign. With the addition of a couple of signings the October, these were the men who were to produce the most successful season ever in t club's history.

e Chelsea programme for
nderland's visit to Stamford
dge on 5 October 1912. This
s the seventh League game of
e season and Sunderland had
l not recorded a win. The
nsioners ran out 2-0 victors
oviding another afternoon of
appointment for the Wearsiders.
arlie Buchan received a kick on
e knee in the first five minutes
d was a passenger on the wing
fore finally being forced to leave
e field. Although the defeat sent
nderland crashing to second off
ttom in the table, from that
int on they never looked back.
the season progressed
nderland stormed up the League
d clinched their fifth League
le.

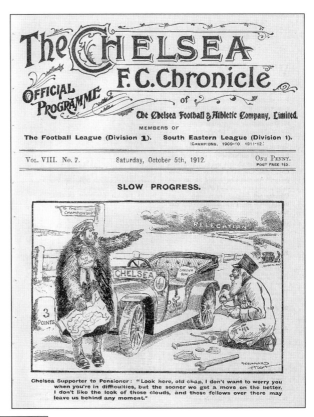

SLOW PROGRESS.

Chelsea Supporter to Pensioner: "Look here, old chap, I don't want to worry you
when you're in difficulties, but the sooner we get a move on the better.
I don't like the look of those clouds, and those fellows over there may
leave us behind any moment."

Making his debut in goal for Sunderland in
the match at Stamford Bridge was Joe Butler.
His transfer from Glossop was the turning
point in Sunderland's fortunes. After the
Chelsea defeat Sunderland won their next
five games, scoring nineteen goals and
conceding only three.

Charlie Gladwin made his debut in the match after the Stamford Bridge defeat. Th physical presence of the barrel-chested full back settled the side and was a major factor in the championship success. The 6ft 1in, 14st former Blackpool man did have one unusual quirk: he overcame the problem of nerves by making himself sick before every game.

A post card of Sunderland's famous Black Cat mascot dating from before the First World War. When Sunderland played Newcastle in an FA Cup tie in March 1909 thousands of supporters made the short journey to St James' Park. The black cat with red and white ribbons attached was much in evidence among the 'invaders'. Sunderland's appearance in the 1913 FA Cup Final was another occasion which brought the lucky feline out in great numbers. The *Football Echo* reported how rail excursions from the area began shortly before midnight with supporters wearing their colours proudly. 'Sunderland's chief mascot was a miniature representation of the black cat, decked out with red and white ribbons, and many scores of these were carried by both sexes.'

ENGLISH CUP FINAL, 1912·13,

PLAYED AT CRYSTAL PALACE.   LONDON,   APRIL 19th, 1913.

CHARLES THOMSON   JOSEPH BACHE

SUNDERLAND v ASTON VILLA

Printed and published by E. MORAN & SONS, Limited, Sunderland.

souvenir brochure of the 1913 FA Cup Final printed in Sunderland. It is now a collector's m and a copy recently changed hands for £700. This publication is sometimes mistaken for e Cup Final programme, which was a much less elaborate work.

After joining Sunderland from Barnsley in 1911 Harry Ness vied with Albert Milton for the left back spot. At times both played together with Ness switching to the other flank. An injury to Milton in the closing stages of the 1912-13 season allowed Ness to play in the semi-final replay and Final at Crystal Palace. By the time the war brought football to a halt he had made the position his own. He returned to play in Sunderland's first League match after the war.

The *London Illustrated News* featured the 1913 FA Cup Final. A huge crowd of 120,081 packed
Crystal Palace to see the top two teams in England contest the Final. A late goal from
Newcastle-born Tommy Barber gave Villa the Cup.

ne of the major talking points of the Final as Charlie Thomson's clash with Villa ntre forward Harry Hampton. Bad feeling tween the pair had started in England-cotland games and carried over into the nal. Although neither was sent off the FA spended both men at the start of the lowing season. The First World War was to ing the curtain down on the Sunderland ipper's career. Even then the club wanted m to return for one more season after the ar. After being demobbed he preferred to sume as landlord at the Black Bull Hotel at estonpans near Edinburgh.

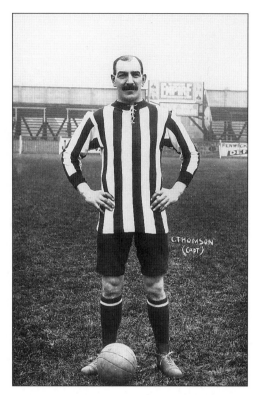

Four days after the Cup Final Walter Tinsley scored the goal in a 1-1 draw at Villa Park that virtually clinched the championship for Sunderland. For the top of the table clash he replaced George Holley who had played in the Final despite not being fully fit. After only a handful more appearances Tinsley was transferred to Exeter City at the end of the following season.

Action from a match in Budapest on Sunderland's tour in the summer of 1913. This was not the first time the Wearsiders had visited the city, four years before they played two games against local opposition winning both matches. This time as reigning League champions there was extra responsibility on their shoulders to put up a good show.

Sunderland played three games in Budapest on the tour. They beat a Budapest XI (9-0) and a Hungary XI (3-2). The third encounter was against Blackburn Rovers who were also touring at that time. Even English opposition proved no obstacle for the Wearsiders. Sunderland finished their tour to the Austro-Hungarian Empire and Germany with a hundred per cent record from seven games.

Welsh international goalkeeper Leigh Richmond Roose joined Sunderland as an amateur in January 1908 having already appeared for Aberystwyth, London Welsh, Everton and Stoke City. He gave an impressive display against Woolwich Arsenal at Plumstead on 21 November 1908. The *Evening Standard* commented on his unique style. 'Roose, if he was tied down, could not explain any one of his methods: they are just methods of Roose. And they are his greatness. He is always Roose. And he is without a superior. No shot is impossible in his way of thinking, no danger too great to run.'

A promotional card given with the *Weekly Courier* bearing a caricature of Roose. Note the goalkeeper's jersey at the time was similar to outfield players. Roose's superb performances when taking over half way through the 1907-08 season were credited with keeping Sunderland up. At the start of the following season he was presented with a testimonial album on behalf of the inhabitants of Sunderland in appreciation of this. At the ceremony he recalled how many had asked what business he had to play for Sunderland, but it was not a business, it was a pleasure. He played for the love of the game and if he could not afford to play for pleasure he would not play at all. He had never played for pay and never would. In the derby match at St James' Park in November 1910 he broke his arm and never played for Sunderland again. He lost his life in the First World War.

Bobby Best scored a hat-trick against Newcastle in the last League derby at St James' Park before the First World War. His goals helped Sunderland to a 5-2 victory on Christmas Day 1914. On a heavily sanded surface the Mickley-on-Tyne youngster scored his first goal after only eight minutes play. His second came on the half hour after holding off the challenge of three United men before slotting the ball home. Shortly after the interval he completed a memorable hat-trick.

Early in his goalkeeping career Walter Scott was known as the 'Penalty King' such was his reputation for saving spot-kicks. Sunderland signed the brilliant 'keeper from Everton for a fee of £750 in the summer of 1911. After being number one choice for most of his first season at the club things began to turn sour during his second campaign. Scott was blamed for a number of defeats and when he missed a training session after a mix up the club suspended him. He was then given a fortnight's notice on the grounds of 'palpable inefficiency'.

nderland's Cup run in 1913 brought Harry
w both joy and disappointment. He was
osen to play for Scotland against Ireland in
blin on 15 March. However, Sunderland
ew a replay with Newcastle and Low
thdrew from the Scotland party to play in
e second replay. He was never selected for
s country again. In contrast brother Wilf
n five caps whilst with Newcastle.

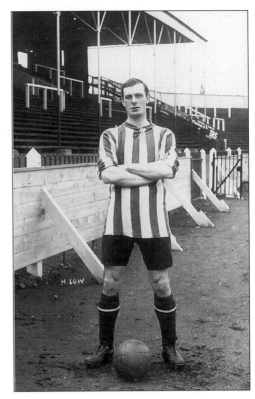

H. LOW

Presented with FOOTBALL SPECIAL, September 30th, 1922.

CHARLIE BUCHAN,
Sunderland's six-foot
star, hasn't had the
caps he deserves, but
is as popular as a Bank
Holiday all over the
country. Weighs 12 st.
6 lbs.

OUR FOOTBALL
BOYS—No. 4.

Yours truly
C. M. Buchan
Sunderland

The gangling figure of Charlie Buchan gave
cartoonists plenty of material to work with.
At the start of his first full season at
Sunderland he stood 5ft 9½in and weighed
10st 5lb. Three months later his weight had
remained the same but he had shot up to
6ft ¾in. This rapid gain in height left him
weak during matches and it also sapped his
confidence. He walked out on Sunderland
and returned to Woolwich. Bob Kyle
persuaded him to return and once he put on
a couple of stones in weight he was back to
his best.

Having finally established himself as first choice left back after his transfer from Barnsley in 1908, Albert Milton looked forward to the 1912-13 season with high hopes. With little over a month of the campaign remaining he had been an ever present in the side, but an injury in the match against Manchester City in 22 Marc 1913 robbed him of an FA Cup Final place and was to effectively signal the end of his Roker career. He received a benefit from th club the following season and then moved on to Swindon. Like former team-mate Roose, the Rotherham-born full back was killed in the war.

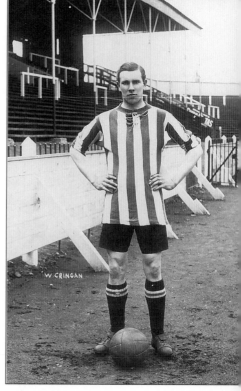

Before the First World War Billy Cringan was just beginning to establish himself in the Sunderland side. In 1915 the club sold him to Celtic to help them through a bad financial patch. With the suspension of the League programme at the end of the 1914-15 season Sunderland could no longer rely on a regular income from gate receipts. After the war Cringan went on to become a Scottish international.

Three

Between the Wars 1919-39

The Cup at last

Joe Kasher signed for Sunderland in May 1919 and was the club's regular centre half in the early post-war seasons. The County Durham man had been a Prisoner of War in Germany for the latter part of hostilities. After returning home Kasher played for Crook Town but appeared as a guest player for Sunderland in the Victory League in 1919. He then played against Sunderland for Crook in the Final of the Durham Senior Cup. Despite being on the wrong end of an 8-0 scoreline Kasher impressed the Sunderland officials and he was signed on.

Frank Cuggy along with Charles Buchan and Jackie Mordue made up the famous 'Sunderland Triangle'. They formed a brilliant understanding on the pitch which led to the trio performing together at international level in Belfast in 1913. Unfortunately the result did not go their way and Ireland recorded their first ever victory over England. However, Cuggy was selected for the corresponding fixture the following year.

The Sunderland squad for the 1919-20 season, the first after the First World War. The Armistice had come too late for the 1918-19 season to get underway but there was a Victory League at the turn of the year. Along with Sunderland seven other local clubs took part. The club made a profit of £2,556 on these games which helped to pay for restoring Roker Park after the neglect of the war years.

Barney Travers scorer of two goals in the first League derby at St James' after the First World War. With a quarter of an hour of the match remaining United led 2-1 when Travers levelled the score. The *Newcastle Daily Journal* reported, 'with five minutes to go Travers got clear away with a great solo effort, and though tackled by McCracken, he scored with a magnificent drive, winning the game for the Wearsiders.' His goals before a crowd of 61,761 earned Sunderland a 3-2 win and completed a double over their old rivals. The previous week the Magpies were beaten by two Charlie Buchan goals at Roker.

The Aston Villa programme for the League encounter with Sunderland on 12 February 1921. Sunderland recorded a 5-1 win over their old rivals with goals from Buchan (2), Marshall (2) and an own goal. Buchan's first goal came after a piece of 'masterful dribbling'. The Sunderland centre forward almost completed a hat-trick as he also struck an upright.

Despite losing four years to the war Charlie Buchan made over four hundred League and Cup appearances for Sunderland. His goalscoring record at Roker was also impressive with better than a goal every two games. In the summer of 1925 Buchan was involved in an extraordinary move to Arsenal. Rather than a set fee Sunderland would receive £2,000 plus £100 for every goal Buchan scored in his first season at Highbury. Fortunately Buchan scored 21 goals and Sunderland, who had wanted £4,000 for the thirty-three-year-old player, received a bonus.

Scottish international centre half Michael Gilhooley was transferred from Hull City on 2 March 1922 for a fee of £5,250. He had an injury-plagued Roker career and only made twenty League appearances in over two years.

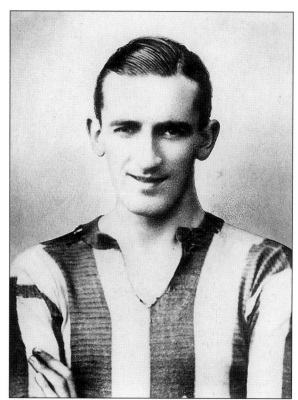

On the same day as Gilhooley signed for Sunderland Jock Paterson joined the club from Leicester City. A free-scoring centre forward Paterson was also a Scottish international at the time. Sunderland's mid-table position prompted manager Bob Kyle to delve into the transfer market.

W. CRESSWELL.

The football world had barely had time to overcome the shock of the double transfer swoop when the following day Sunderland signed Warney Cresswell. South Shields were paid £5,500 for the England full back. All three newcomers made their debut in the game against Sheffield United at Roker on 4 March. The new blood helped Sunderland to a 1-0 victory with the goal coming from 'old boy' Charlie Buchan.

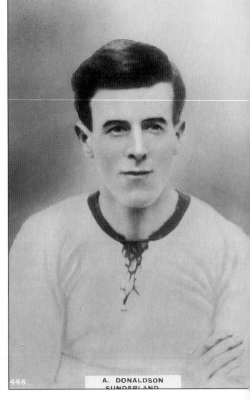

446   A. DONALDSON
                       SUNDERLAND

The big money spending had still not been completed: at the end of March Alex Donaldson was bought from Bolton Wanderers. The Scottish international winger was to play only one full season at Sunderland before moving on to Manchester City. Sunderland had spent over £20,000 in a month but of the international quartet only Cresswell was to prove a long-term success at Roker.

Copyright Arthur Hackett. SUNDERLAND A.F.C., 1922-23. 40 Grey St., Newcastle-on-Tyne.

FERGUSON. CRESSWELL. ENGLAND. ROBSON. HAWES. POOLE.
R. H. KYLE (Sec.). DONALDSON. BUCHAN. PARKER (Capt.). PATERSON. ELLIS. W. WILLIAMS (Trainer)

The Sunderland squad in the 1922-23 season which finished runners-up to Liverpool for the championship. The strike force of Buchan and Paterson was to prove a lethal combination. Buchan's 30 League goals made him the country's leading marksman. Paterson contributed another 21 goals to Sunderland's total of 72.

Centre forward Paterson looks on as the Blackburn keeper Davis claims the ball in the match at Ewood Park on 23 September 1922. In his first full season after leaving Leicester Paterson finished with a total of 24 League and Cup goals. This was to be the high point of his Roker career, in October 1924 he was transferred to Preston North End.

51

Charlie Parker closes in on a Blackburn Rovers player in the same match at Ewood Park in 1922. Record signing from South Shields, Warney Cresswell looks on. Two other expensive acquisitions – Jock Paterson and Alex Donaldson were also in the side that drew 0-0 with Rovers.

Left: Ernie England is beaten to the ball by a Chelsea player. The Sunderland full back was an ever present during the 1922-23 season. Calls for him to be recognised at international level went unheeded. Right: Soaring above the Chelsea defence Charlie Buchan heads for goal.

Sunderland's Billy Moore can claim to have played before the biggest crowd in history. In 1912 he joined the club from Seaton Delaval on amateur forms. He made his League debut against Sheffield United on 7 February 1914. In that year he travelled with the England Amateur team on two Continental tours. He scored two goals on his debut in a 8-1 win over Belgium in Brussels and in two games against Sweden in Stockholm he found the net three times. After appearing in a defeat in Denmark he ended his amateur career and signed professional with Sunderland in August 1914. He was beginning to make his way in the first team when the war halted matters. After the resumption he returned to Roker Park but could never establish a regular place in the side. In May 1922 Sunderland transferred him to West Ham United and within a year he was turning out in the first Wembley Cup Final against Bolton Wanderers.

The official attendance for the 1923 Cup Final was 127,000 but some estimates put the figure as high as a quarter of a million. People continued to surge through the gates long after the capacity had been reached. The huge crowd was forced on to the pitch and the start was delayed. Despite finishing up on the losing side at Wembley Billy Moore's new career continued to flourish when he played for England. After his playing days were over he became West Ham's trainer and stayed at the club up to 1960.

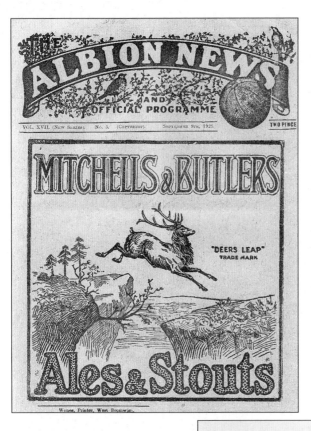

The West Bromwich Albion programme for Sunderland's League visit on 5 September 1925. Sunderland had made an impressive start to the season with home wins over Birmingham (3-1) and Blackburn Rovers (6-2). This continued at the Hawthorns with Dave Halliday notching a hat-trick and Coglin and Ellis also each finding the net in a 5-2 victory. The next game brought a 6-1 win against Sheffield United at Roker but then more erratic form set in. Sunderland eventually finished the season in third place in the League.

Sunderland's good form owed much to Dave Halliday who scored ten goals in the first four games of the season. He finished the 1925-26 season with 38 League goals with a further four in the FA Cup. The Scottish centre forward still holds the Sunderland record for the most League goals in one season. His 43 goals in the 1928-29 campaign also made him the country's leading goalscorer.

...ell in the Sunderland goal comes under pressure from Manchester United's attack during a ...eague match at Roker Park on 30 November 1929. At this time Sunderland were in a period ...f transition, with manager Johnny Cochrane having taken over only the previous season.

...he Sunderland 'keeper had a busy afternoon despite the home side taking an early lead ...rough Gunson. After Joe Spence equalised Manchester United took control with Spence ...oring a second and Hanson and Ball stretching the lead. Morrison pulled a late goal back to ...ake the final score 4-2 to United.

An unusual picture of Sunderland's line-up before the start of the 1930-31 season. Left to right: Billy Eden, Billy Clunas, Tommy Urwin, Bill Murray, Bobby Gurney, Jock McDougall, Paddy Bell, Patsy Gallacher, Harold Shaw, Arthur Andrews, Jimmy Connor. The only change in the team that opened the campaign with a 3-3 draw at home to Manchester City was Bob Robinson replaced Bell in goal.

The Portsmouth programme for the League match with Sunderland on 6 September 1930. The third game of the season was to produce Sunderland's third draw. If a return of only a point a game was a disappointment, worse was to follow – five successive defeats. Despite these set-backs Sunderland ended the season in a respectable mid-table position.

Sunderland's Scottish international goalkeeper Bob Middleton in action at Stamford Bridge in 1930. The legendary Hughie Gallacher was the star of the show when Sunderland visited the capital for a League game on 13 December. Having signed from Newcastle only a few months before Scotland's diminutive centre forward scored two of Chelsea's goals in a 5-0 drubbing.

When Bill Murray joined Sunderland in April 1927 from Cowdenbeath he had no idea that he would spend all but two of the next thirty years at Roker Park. After nine years as the club's right back he moved back to Scotland with St Mirren. In 1938 he returned to take over from Johnny Cochrane as manager. He resigned in 1957 having just failed on a number of occasions to bring silverware to the club.

Before joining Sunderland from Aberdeen Benny Yorston had been compared with the great Hughie Gallacher. He had topped the Scottish League goalscoring charts in the 1929-30 season with 38 goals in 38 games. Sunderland paid £2,000 to lure the 5ft 5in Scottish international to Roker in January 1932. Despite scoring seven goals in his first five games for Sunderland Yorston's stay was to be brief. Fierce competition for places in the forward line from men like Gurney, Gallacher and Carter made him surplus t requirements and he was allowed to move on to Middlesbrough.

In February 1930 Sunderland were chasing the signature of Harold Shaw of Wolves when Newcastle made an inquiry. Wolves upped the price and Sunderland had to pay a record fee for a left back – £7,000. Ironically Shaw made his debut in the derby at St James' Park on 22 February. Despite a brilliant individual performance from the new signing Sunderland went down to a 3-0 defeat.

The West Bromwich goalkeeper drops on the ball as Bobby Gurney is about to shoot for goal. The League game at Roker Park on 11 September 1935 ended in a 6-1 Sunderland victory. The star of a brilliant performance was Raich Carter who notched four goals.

After signing from Bradford Park Avenue in April 1932 Bert Davis only missed five League games in the next three seasons. He was in and out of the 1935-36 championship-winning side but still scored 10 goals. The low point of that season came in the match against Middlesbrough at Ayresome Park. Raich Carter was sent off for the only time in his career and when Davis said something to the referee he followed him for an early bath.

The Birmingham City programme for Sunderland's visit on 13 April 1936. A brilliant 7-2 victory ensured Sunderland claimed the First Division title. The score could have been much higher as the home 'keeper made a dozen outstanding saves. The *Newcastle Journal* correspondent reported, 'I have had nearly 40 years of first class football, but I have never seen a team toyed with to the extent Birmingham were in this match.'

Bobby Gurney scorer of four goals at St Andrews which helped Sunderland equal Aston Villa's record of six titles received a special welcome on his return to Wearside. A crowd of 50,000 awaited the players arrival home. When the team emerged from the Central Railway Station there were shouts of 'Next Year Bobby' referring to the FA Cup being the next target. After joining Sunderland from Bishop Auckland in 1925 Bobby went on to become one of the club's all-time greats. His whole-hearted centre forward play was rewarded with over two hundred League and Cup goals. His displays were also recognised at international level winning an England cap against Scotland.

rrow-born Jimmy Thorpe
agically died four days after being
jured in a League game against
helsea in 1936. The young
alkeeper received kicks to the
ad and body in a goalmouth
ramble at Roker Park on
turday, 1 February. Although
zed he finished the match but
ok ill on the Monday. He was
ken to hospital but lapsed into a
ma and died on the Wednesday.
he twenty-two-year-old suffered
m diabetes but the coroner said
e rough treatment contributed to
s death.

nderland with the 1935-36 championship trophy. Back row: Carter, Thomson, Hall,
apson, Hastings, Collin, Clarke. Front row: Cochrane (manager), Davis, Gurney, Gallacher,
onnor, Reid (trainer).

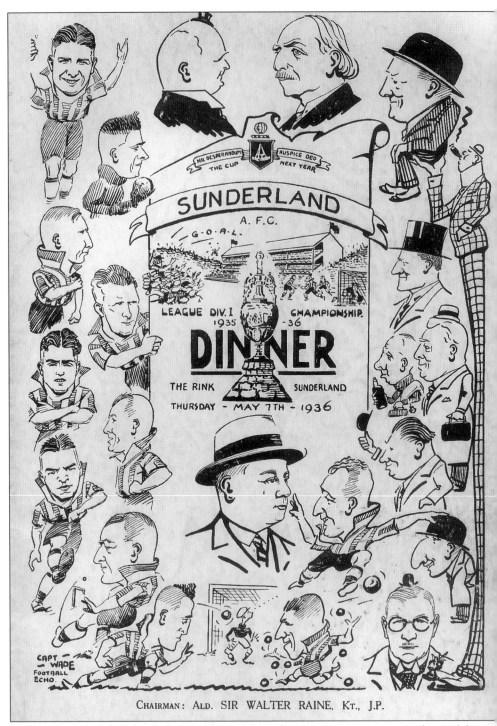

The Town Council honoured the 1935-36 championship-winning team with a celebration dinner at the New Rink. Vice-chairman Duncan White presented the players with the winners' medals before 350 guests. There was an emotional moment when he called up Jimmy Thorpe's father to receive his son's medal.

n aerial view of Roker Park in 1936. At the time the old Clockstand (left) was being rebuilt.
rchibald Leitch was the architect, the same man who had designed the Main Stand (right) a
w years before. Almost thirty years later a roof was put over the Fulwell End (top). The
oncrete supports of the Roker End (bottom) became structurally unsafe in 1982 and had to be
artially demolished.

he Sunderland team dressed in the height of 1930s fashion pose under the Roker End.
etween 1912 and 1913 the Roker End had been erected at a cost of £20,000. The massive
oncrete supports were an innovation as up to then terracing was cut from earth banking or
uilt on wood or steel supports. In 1902 twenty-six people had died when wooden terracing
ollapsed at Ibrox Park during an England-Scotland game.

Scottish international inside forward Patsy Gallacher was a great favourite of the Roker crowd. His goal in the semi-final against Millwall put Sunderland into the Final. In November 1938 the twenty-eight-year-old was transferred to Stoke for £5,500. He had just received his second benefit cheque for £650 from Sunderland, having completed ten years with the club. He thought a change of surroundings would do him good.

Sandy McNab was the only change from the semi-final side to that which turned out at Wembley. Alex Hastings was the unlucky man to lose out, he had been injured in a game just before the Cup run began. Fellow Scot McNab then played in all seven Cup games up to the semi.

Sunderland supporter takes a break in the streets of ondon on Cup Final Day 1937. Sunderland's allocation as limited to just 10,000 tickets. Roker Park was undated with postal applications at least four times that amber. Some supporters had followed the team in every und. Long journeys to Southampton, Luton, olverhampton, Sheffield and Huddersfield, counted for thing. Even a number of season ticket holders were too te with their applications and missed out. For weeks the cal press was full of correspondence on the subject. amours of Cup tickets abounded on Wearside in the run to the Final. Roker and Fulwell British Legion had a tter published in the *Echo* denying they had received a tch of 200 tickets from Sunderland AFC. They declared ey had received absolutely none.

n unusual shot of Sunderland's team prior to going to Wembley. Who are the Sunderland ayers doing the Ravanelli impersonations almost sixty years before the Italian striker arrived n Teesside? Answers on the next page.

Back row: Hall, Thomson (partly hidden), Hastings, Carter, Gurney. Middle: Johnston, Burbanks, McNab. Front: Gorman, Mapson, Duns.

Just before the kick-off 2s 6d ($12\frac{1}{2}$p) tickets were changing hands for 15s (75p). All but 1,800 of Sunderland's 10,000 allocation were for tickets under 5s (25p). At the upper end of the market guinea (£1.05) tickets were fetching £5 5s (£5.25). Preston North End had the same allocation of tickets as Sunderland yet the crowd numbered 93,495.

The 1937 FA Cup Final programme. Sunderland's path to the Final was not without its jitters. The quarter-final clash with Wolves was an epic struggle. A 1-1 draw at Molineux was followed by a 2-2 stalemate at Roker. In the decider at Hillsborough goals from Carter, Gurney, Gallacher and Thomson finally eased Sunderland into the semi.

FINAL TIE

OF THE
FOOTBALL
ASSOCIATION
CHALLENGE CUP
COMPETITION

AT THE

EMPIRE STADIUM
WEMBLEY

SATURDAY, MAY 1, 1937

CORONATION YEAR OF THEIR MAJESTIES
KING GEORGE VI AND QUEEN ELIZABETH

PRESTON NORTH END
v.
SUNDERLAND
Kick-off 3 p.m.

OFFICIAL PROGRAMME SIXPENCE

The Sunderland goal under intense pressure from the Preston attack in the 1937 Final. On this occasion they managed to get the ball clear. The defence was breached before the interval when Scottish international Frank O'Donnell put Preston ahead.

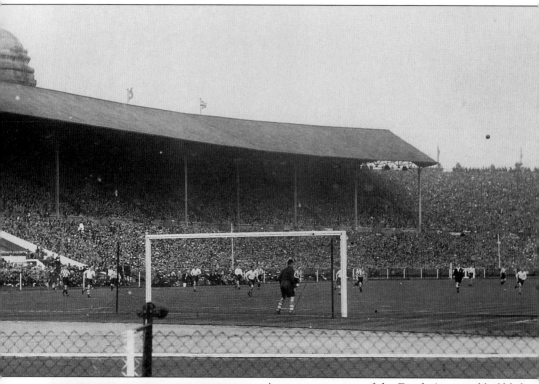

SUNDERLAND

A panoramic view of the Final. A second half fight back saw Sunderland score three times without reply. A Gurney header pulled the sides level and then goals from Carter and Burbanks sealed Sunderland's triumph. Note the old roof only covered the seated area of the ground. Improvements completed for the 1966 World Cup included a new roof which sheltered all spectators from the elements.

Sunderland's Black Cat was depicted in a series of cigarette cards in 1933. The reverse of the card noted that even at that time Sunderland were less gloriously known as the 'Wearsiders' or the 'Rokerites'. Twelve-year-old Sunderland supporter Billy Morris smuggled a black kitten into the 1937 Final to help bring his favourites luck. The red and white adorned cat stayed in the youngster's coat pocket during the game.

The Roker Roar on tour
1937 style. A supporter
down for the Final shows
that fancy dress at
Sunderland matches is not a
modern day phenomenon.

A crucial factor in Sunderland's Cup
win was the performance of Bert
Johnston against the Preston number
nine. Although Frank O'Donnell
scored in the first half the
Sunderland centre half had his
measure for most of the game. When
his playing days were over Johnston
remained at Roker Park by joining
the training staff.

The Queen congratulates Raich Carter before presenting him with the trophy that had for so long been a stumbling block for Sunderland. The Sunderland skipper, who a few day before had been married, received a special message when handed the Cup. The Queen said, 'That is a nice wedding present for you.'

SUNDERLAND CUP TEAM 1936-37.

THOMSON. GORMAN. JOHNSTON. MAPSON. HALL. HASTINGS.
JOHN COCHRANE. CARTER. GURNEY. GALLACHER. A. REID.
(SEC. MANAGER.)   (TRAINER.)
DUNS.   ARTHUR HACKETT   BURBANKS.
                     Copyright
                  J.C.   8

The Sunderland eleven that beat Millwall 2-1 in the 1937 FA Cup semi-final at Huddersfield Sandy McNab replaced Alex Hastings for the Final.

The celebrations begin: Left to right: Billy Dunlop (assistant trainer), Jimmy Gorman, Andy Reid (trainer), Len Duns, Raich Carter with the Cup, Sandy McNab and Bert Johnston.

A composite photograph of the team with the FA Cup. Sunderland included five Scotsmen in the Wembley side. Another Scot in the Preston side was to become even more famous as a manager – Bill Shankly.

Sunday Graphic and Sunday News, May 2, 1937.

TRUTH ABOUT BUDGET PANIC:
By BEVERLEY
BAXTER, M.P.

SUNDAY GRAPHIC
and SUNDAY NEWS

BEAUTY
FOR ALL:
GREAT
NEW
SERIES
RADIO P. 28

No. 1,152.   [Registered as a newspaper.]   SUNDAY, MAY 2, 1937.   TWOPENCE.

HIS FINAL WEDDING GIFT
The Queen Presents The Cup to Sunderland's Captain

Sunderland's cup victory made front page news the day after the Final. Despite having won six
League titles, losing finalists in 1913 had been the closest Sunderland had been to winning the
FA Cup.

The Sunderland and Celtic teams for the friendly at Roker Park on 6 October 1937. The Scottish Cup-holders beat their English counterparts by a score of 2-0. One of the goalscorers was Jimmy McGrory who was to retire the following year after scoring a record 550 goals in first-class football. McGrory's goalscoring record for Celtic was phenomenal: in 378 League games he scored 397 goals. In contrast to Sunderland's solitary Cup win at that time Celtic had won their competition on no less than fifteen occasions. The Sunderland and Celtic teams together with the English and Scottish Cups. Back row: Gorman, Delaney, McDowall, Crum, Burbanks, Murphy. Third row: Reid (trainer), Hall, Hogg, Mapson, Peterson, Doyle, McDonald, Johnston, McMenemy (trainer). Second row: Johnny Cochrane (manager), Gurney, McGrory, Carter, Lyon, Gallacher, Maley (manager). Front row: Duns, Buchan, Thomson, Morrison. The Celtic players had watched Sunderland's victory at Wembley in recognition of their Cup triumph the previous week. Despite Sunderland having a large Scottish contingent in their ranks the Celtic players were supporting their opponents in the Final. Former Celtic men Frank and Hugh O'Donnell were in the Preston side that day.

Arsenal goalkeeper Boulton beats Bobby Gurney to the ball in the League match at Highbury on 18 September 1937 before a 60,000 crowd. In the corresponding fixture three seasons before Sunderland's visit had set Arsenal's record attendance. With the Gunners chasing their third successive League title, 73,295 had packed Highbury for the match.

oulton again foils the Sunderland attack, this time Raich Carter comes off second best. The
atch produced an amazing goalscoring burst. Milne put Arsenal ahead after three minutes
lay and within five minutes were 4-0 up. England centre forward Ted Drake, Hulme and
avidson all found the net. Only a further two minutes had passed when Bobby Gurney pulled
goal back. The star-studded Arsenal and Sunderland sides could not add to the scoreline in
e remaining 75 minutes.

underland 'keeper Matt Middleton saves a shot from Milne. The Gunners' line-up for the
atch included eight England internationals: Drake, Bastin, Hulme, Copping, Roberts,
rayston, Hapgood and Male.

The Tottenham programme on the occasion of the record-breaking gate at White Hart Lane on 5 March 1938. Cup holders Sunderland stood between Spurs and a semi-final spot. On a warm sunny afternoon 75,038 crammed into the stadium with over 10,000 locked out.

The Spurs defence comes under pressure from one of the most feared attacks in the country during the Cup tie. It was the Londoners third successive appearance in the quarter-finals.

purs' goalkeeper Hooper and defender Hall repel a Sunderland attack in the record-breaking Cup tie at White Hart Lane.

Gibbons of Spurs gets in a shot on the Sunderland goal but Mapson clears. Sunderland had gone twelve games undefeated in the competition before the Tottenham game and the thirteenth was not to prove unlucky. A great goal from Raich Carter ten minutes from time settled the issue.

Four

Wartime
1939-45

Phoney war to real bombs on Roker Park

Eddie Burbanks scored in Sunderland's last League game before the war. The match at Highbury on 2 September 1939 was put back to a 5 p.m. kick-off because of traffic congestion. The day before the task of evacuating three million mothers, children and the disabled from the large cities had got underway. The game itself was a rout with Ted Drake scoring four goals in a 5-1 Arsenal win. The following day Britain declared war on Germany and the League programme ended for the duration.

Birkenhead-born Johnny Mapson was signed from Reading a month after Jimmy Thorpe's tragic death. He made the keeper's jersey his own until the war brought a halt to proceedings. The former Reading 'keeper toured South Africa in the summer of 1939 with an England party. He played in two Test matches against the Springboks, winning 8-2 in Durban and 2-1 in Johannesburg. Mapson appeared for England in a wartime international against Wales on 26 April 1941. The game at Nottingham ended in a 4-1 victory to England.

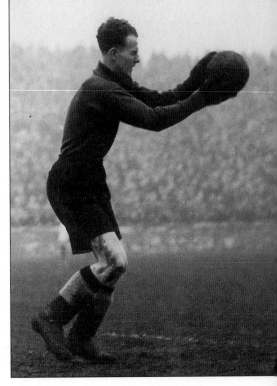

efore the war Raich Carter won
very honour in the game with
underland. After serving in the
Auxiliary Fire Service for two
ears at the start of the war
Carter moved on to the RAF. In
December 1945 he joined Derby
County with whom he found
immediate success. In his first
eason he helped the Rams to an
A Cup Final victory at
Wembley. In March 1948 he set
ut on a new challenge as player-
ssistant manager at Hull City.

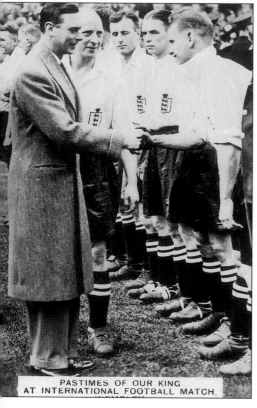

PASTIMES OF OUR KING
AT INTERNATIONAL FOOTBALL MATCH.

The Duke of York (later George VI)
meets Raich Carter and the rest of the
England players before an international.
The England captain doing the
introductions was Tommy 'Snowy'
Cooper who was to die in a motor cycle
crash while serving with the Military
Police in 1940. Despite winning thirteen
full caps Carter's international career was
decimated by the war. He won the last of
his six caps whilst with Sunderland on
17 April 1937. It was to be almost ten
years before he made his next appearance
now playing for Derby. He wasted no
time in resurrecting his England career
playing in the first seven full
internationals after the war.

Action from the first leg of the War League Cup Final against Wolves at Roker Park on 23 Ma
1942. This competition had replaced the FA Cup which had been suspended for the duration
A crowd of 32,113 saw Sunderland held to a 2-2 draw by the Midlanders. One of Sunderland
scorers was Newcastle United's Albert Stubbins who was playing as a guest. Stubbins was th
leading marksmen in wartime football in England with well over two hundred goals. Stubbin
haul included a remarkable run of four hat-tricks in succession.

olves 'keeper Sidlow manages to keep the ball out during the first leg game at Roker. Raich arter found the net in the first match and the England international also scored in the second at Molineux before 43,038 people. However, this was not enough as Wolves ran out 4-1 nners to lift the trophy.

A photograph from the Luftwaffe archives shows how perilous Roker Park's location was in terms of 'targets' such as Sunderland's shipyards and docks.

An air raid on 16 May 1943 caused damage to the pitch and also to the Main Stand. The old club house on the corner of Roker Baths Road was destroyed. A special constable was killed in a street near the ground. After a raid a couple of months before when a bomb also landed on the pitch the German High Command announced, 'on the night of March 14, a formation of fast bomber aircraft made a strong attack against the shipbuilding centre of Sunderland.'

Colonel Joe Prior served as Sunderland chairman during the war years. The Colonel had fought in both the Boer War and the First World War. When he travelled to Scotland with manager Bob Kyle intending to buy a player, he bought a horse. First appointed to the board in 1919 he served the club for thirty years. A well-known figure on Wearside his name lives on in the Colonel Prior public house at Doxford Park.

Left to right: Arthur Wright, Len Duns and Arthur Housam. The locally-born trio all had the Roker careers interrupted by the war. They all played wartime football with Sunderland an then resumed playing League football after hostilities. Between September 1939 and the end the war forty Sunderland players had joined the forces. Many former players also served, lil Johnny Lynas who made a number of appearances for Sunderland in 1928-29 season. He w taken prisoner by the Japanese at the fall of Singapore and worked in a Prisoner of War hospit in Thailand for the rest of the war.

Five

Bank of England Club 1946-58

Money can't buy success

Eddie Burbanks in action against Manchester United. Old Trafford was severely damag[ed] during air raids and United shared Maine Road with rivals City for a period after the war. It w[as] while at their temporary home that United set the all-time attendance record for a League gar[me] – 83,260 for the visit of Arsenal in January 1948. Having scored in the last game before the w[ar] Burbanks also found the mark in Sunderland's first League game after the resumption. [He] scored in Sunderland's 3-2 victory over Derby County seven years after the Arsenal game.

inderland's team for the League visit to Bramall Lane on 11 October 1947. Back row: Scotson,
right, Stelling, Mapson, Hudgell, Walsh. Front row: Duns, Robinson, Davis, Watson,
eynolds. In the early part of the game a number of Sunderland passes went to the red and
hite stripes of United instead of to unfamiliar white-shirted team-mates. Despite this
inderland led 2-0 at half-time through goals from Davis and Reynolds. The home side stormed
ck to earn a 3-2 victory, with the United 'keeper saving a Reynolds penalty.

posite: Old and New Boys: Left to right: Len Duns, Tommy McLain, W. Cook (trainer),
d Hall, Len Shackleton. Duns had been with Sunderland since 1933 while the other three
yers were all post-war signings.

Johnny Mapson in action during a Sunderland-Chelsea game at Stamford Bridge in 1947. In November 1945 82,000 people crammed into the ground for the visit of Moscow Dynamo. With the gates locked many spectators took up precarious positions on the roof. In 1955 it was Roker Park's turn to entertain the famous Russian club.

Sunderland's Ronnie Turnbull made one of the most sensational debuts in Football League history. When he was chosen for the game against Portsmouth at Roker Park on November 1947 he could not have dared dream of the eventual outcome. After twenty minutes he scored his first goal, followed by another ten minutes later. Early in the second half he completed his hat-trick. Pompey pulled a goal back but the debut-boy had the last word when he scored his fourth shortly before the final whistle. Despite finding the net again in his next match the goal flood was then reduced to a trickle. In September 1949 he was transferred to Manchester City.

pporters stream across the Wearmouth Bridge after the match against Arsenal on 18 ptember 1948. A crowd of 64,436 had set new League attendance figures for Roker Park. e record was not to last long, Blackpool's visit the following season surpassed the nners' total.

nderland squad at the start of the 1949-50 season. Back row: Scarth, R. Robinson, Clurkie, Mapson, McLain. Second row: Jones (third team trainer), Gray (senior trainer), ver, Davis, Marston, Ramsden, Hall, Scotson, A. Wright, Hudgell, Johnston (reserve ner). Third row: J. Robinson, Turnbull, Broadis, Duns, Bill Murray (manager), Stelling, Shackleton, Dunn, Walsh. Front row: J. Shackleton, Dougall, T. Wright.

Derby County 'keeper Townsend takes the ball off Tommy Wright in the match at Roker Pa
on 21 January 1950. A crowd of 62,413 gathered to see if Sunderland could maintain their tit
challenge. During the season over one million people attended matches at Roker Park.

Johnny Mapson holds off a challenge from Derby's Morris. Sunderland ran out easy 6-1 winne
with Dickie Davis notching a hat-trick. Going into the final month of the season Sunderla
were favourites to lift the title. But a home defeat against lowly Manchester City was to co
Sunderland the championship.

Sunderland players and officials boarding a chartered plane at London Airport bound for Istanbul in May 1950. A party from Hull City shared the flight, with the players from both clubs having to be insured for £1,000,000 for the journey.

On the journey to Turkey the Sunderland party had an overnight stop-over in Rome. Len Shackleton recalled how the peace of the night was broken with the sound of breaking glass. His fear of an anti-British attack on the hotel were eased when he discovered team-mate Reg Scotson was the cause of the commotion. He had opened one of the windows and not realising it was double glazed put his head through the second pane. Reg survived the incident without any serious injury.

Johnny Mapson goes in bravely against the Galatasaray captain in the third game of t
Turkish tour. In the first match Len Shackleton scored a hat-trick against Besiktas before a se
out crowd of 25,000.

Shackleton, ball and goalkeeper all end up in the Galatasaray net on the way to a 4-3 victc
Sunderland not only finished the tour with a hundred per cent record but their style of footb
won many friends. After the last match the Turks said they had been given lessons in the gar
by 'masters of football'.

On returning from Turkey Willie Watson discovered he had been selected for England's World Cup party for Brazil. A stylish footballer who could play in a variety of positions, Willie was one of the game's gentlemen. As well as representing his country at football he also played Test cricket.

Sunderland team in the 1950-51 season. Back row: Gray (trainer), A. Wright, Hall, McLain, Mapson, Ford, Shackleton, Walsh. Front row: T. Wright, Davis, Hedley, Hudgell.

The Sunderland and Galatasaray teams line up before a friendly at Roker Park on 11 September 1950. Four months before the Istanbul club had played hosts to Sunderland. A crowd of 14,830 turned out with the hope of seeing some 'Eastern promise'.

Sunderland skipper Len Duns receives a pennant from his opposite number of Galatasaray before the kick-off. Sunderland again proved too strong for the Turkish side, goals from Kirtley Duns and Davis completed a comfortable 3-1 victory.

he eighteen-year-old Galatasaray 'keeper Turgay Seren in action at Roker. The youngster
ent on to become a big star in Turkish football, playing for his country on more than fifty
ccasions.

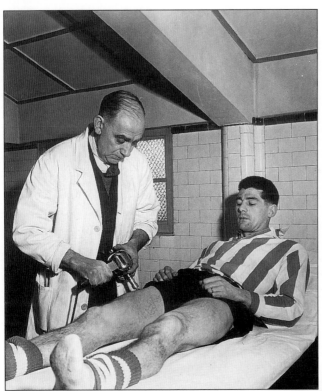

Trevor Ford on the treatment table. Alex Wilson, the former Arsenal goalkeeper, was Sunderland's first qualified physiotherapist. Up to that time the job of treating injuries fell to the trainer. As early as 1930 there was a special treatment room at Roker Park with 'sun-ray' equipment to 'tone up the system'.

Trevor Ford is presented with a Welsh cap in the Roker dressing-room as team-mates Len Shackleton and Willie Watson look on. On 15 November 1950 Ford appeared in an international against England at Roker Park. Despite scoring two goals Ford still ended up on the losing side. England ran out 4-2 winners.

ackpool's Mudie miskicks his effort on goal and Hedley manages to clear in the League match
Bloomfield Road on 20 January 1951. Sunderland supporters always looked forward to visits
Blackpool to sample the non-football entertainment on offer (even in winter).

nderland's Billy Walsh and Brown of Blackpool challenge for the ball in the same match. Goals
om Dickie Davis and Trevor Ford earned Sunderland a 2-2 draw against the Seasiders.

The one and only Len Shackleton. Sunderland broke the transfer record when they paid Newcastle £20,050 to bring his extraordinary talent to Roker Park in 1948. On Christmas Day 1940 Shackleton recorded the unusual feat of playing two matches for two different clubs. On the morning he played for Bradford Park Avenue against Leeds United at Elland Road. Then in the afternoon he turned out for Bradford City at Huddersfield. Wartime regulations allowed players to appear as guests for different clubs.

The 'Clown Prince of Soccer' in England shirt and cap. Only five full caps was poor reward for such a brilliant footballer. After making his debut against Denmark in a 0-0 draw in September 1948 Shack was on the winning side in every international appearance he made after. The last of these was a 3-1 victory over reigning World champions West Germany in December 1954.

upporters who turned up at Roker Park for the FA Cup tie against Southampton on 27 January 951 were greeted by the unusual sight of Sunderland turning out in black and white stripes. ecause of a clash of colours the FA ruled that both teams had to change with Sunderland orrowing a set of strips from neighbours Newcastle.

ohnny Mapson beats Bates of Southampton to the ball in the Fourth Round tie. A brace of oals from Dickie Davis settled the issue. After beating Norwich in the next round Sunderland dvanced into the quarter-finals. Wolves gained a 1-1 draw at Roker and then won the replay at 1olineux 3-1.

Raich Carter leads out Hull City against the club where he first made his name. The teams met for the East Riding Invitation Trophy at Boothferry Park on 28 April 1952. This was played annually by Hull City who invited Sunderland to mark a very special occasion – Raich Carter's last game before retiring from football.

After the game most of the near 30,000 crowd gathered on the pitch in front of the grandstand. The man who had led Hull to the Third Division title and had helped save them from relegation was given a rapturous reception. The match itself had ended in a 2-2 draw, after the home side had been 2-0 up. Two goals from Trevor Ford in the last quarter of an hour levelled the score.

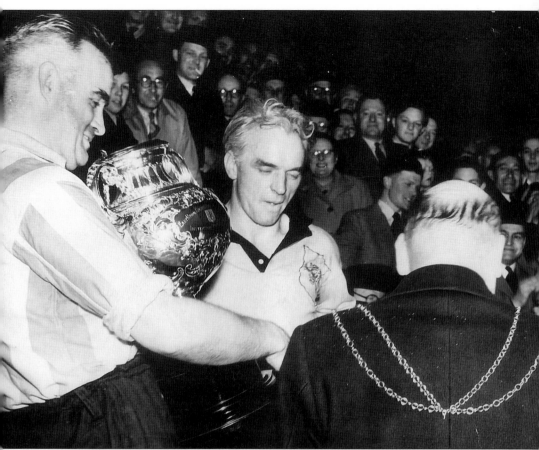

Because the teams had drawn the captains tossed a coin to see who would keep the trophy for the first six months. Fred Hall called correctly and the trophy's first port of call was Roker Park. Although billed as Raich Carter's last game it was to prove not to be so. In January 1953 he was ~ured out of retirement to play for Cork Athletic and helped them to win the FA of Ireland ~up.

Fred Hall leads out the Sunderland side for the first match under Roker Park's new floodlights on 10 December 1952. Sunderland played in what were described as 'flame coloured luminous shirts'. The opposition for the occasion was provided by Dundee. The star of the visitor's team was Billy Steel who cost £23,000 (double the previous Scottish record) when bought from Derby County two years before. Steel had scored four goals in a match against Northern Ireland the previous month.

A crowd of 34,352 were treated to a great night of football with Sunderland eventually running out 5-3 victors. Although the cost of installing the 75 pylons and arc lamps ran into thousands of pounds the running costs were tiny in comparison with those of today. Sunderland paid no more than £1 for the electricity for the Dundee game in 1952. A spokesman for NEEB at the time said the floodlights used energy costing 7s 6d an hour. Club secretary George Crow commented, 'it was like a Technicolour film... I think we have got a real success here.' At the Football League annual meeting in the summer of 1955 Sunderland proposed that postponed matches should be played under floodlights. The proposal was adopted despite the fact many clubs at the time still did not have floodlights.

Welsh international Ray Daniel was a £27,000 signing from Arsenal in the 1953 close season. At the time Daniel said, 'I had nothing to do with deciding how much Sunderland would pay, but I will not be happy until Sunderland supporters are saying "He's worth every penny of it".' Whilst with the Gunners Daniel played for Wales against England at Roker Park in November 1950. During his stay at Sunderland he continued to be selected for his country and went on to win a total of 21 caps.

Tommy Wright gets down low to head for goal in a friendly against Third Lanark at Roker Park. Sunderland had paid the Scottish club £20,000 for the services of George Aitken in November 1951. Both Wright and Aitken won Scottish caps during their time at Roker.

Sunderland's programme for Bolton's League visit to Roker Park on Easter Monday 1953. Two goals from Tommy Wright gave Sunderland a 2-0 victory. This avenged a 5-0 defeat against Wanderers at Burnden Park on the Good Friday.

Tommy Wright's performances on the right wing, centre forward or inside forward earned him three caps for Scotland. In January 1955 he moved back north when he joined East Fife as part of the deal that brought Charlie Fleming to Roker. By coincidence Wright and Fleming had played together as youngsters for Fifeshire side Blairhall Colliery.

Tommy Wright in action against the famous gold and black of Wolverhampton Wanderers at Molineux. Wright enjoyed playing against Wolves: in six League meetings he scored four goals.

The Wolves 'keeper acrobatically saves from Tommy Wright at Roker Park. During the 1950s the Molineux club were one of the top sides in the country. Under inspirational skipper Billy Wright they won the championship three times during the decade. Fixtures between the clubs were so popular they were often arranged for the Christmas or New Year period.

Ray Daniel sends Manchester City 'keeper Savage the wrong way from the penalty spot in the match at Maine Road on 8 September 1956. The 62nd minute goal came too late as City were already 3-0 up and held on to the final whistle. The scoreline would have been even heavier if it had not been for Johnny Bollands' brilliant display in the Sunderland goal. One of City's goalscorers was Don Revie who was to join Sunderland only two months later.

Sunderland goalkeeper Johnny Bollands at full stretch. He faced stiff competition for the goalkeeper's jersey from Scottish international Willie Fraser. The result was that he was limited to sixty-one League appearances in a four year Roker career.

Ray Daniel gets in an effort on the Manchester United goal in the League meeting at Roker Park on 13 October 1956. Left to right: Duncan Edwards, Ted Purdon, Ray Daniel, Mark Jones, Bill Foulkes and Eddie Colman. United were the reigning League champions with an outstanding young team. Twenty-year-old Duncan Edwards was already a legend in the game having become the youngest player to win an England cap eighteen months before. A 3-1 win at Roker helped them retain the title but it turned out to be a poignant occasion as it was the last time the Busby Babes played at Sunderland. In February 1958 the plane carrying the United team back from a European Cup tie crashed on take-off. Eight United players were killed, including Edwards, Jones and Colman. Centre half Bill Foulkes survived and was in the team that won the European Cup at Wembley ten years later.

At the time of the Munich Air Disaster Ernie Taylor was due to join Sunderland from Blackpool. Because of United's dire straits the Sunderland directors allowed the little inside right to go to Old Trafford. At the end of 1958, once the immediate crisis was over, Taylor eventually joined his hometown club.

Six

More 'Downs' than 'Ups' 1958-73

Relegations then Cup Dream

Charlie Hurley was one of the greatest players ever to wear the famous red and white Sunderland shirt. Yet he could hardly have had a worse baptism to his Roker career. After 7-0 and 6-0 defeats at Blackpool and Burnley respectively, the young centre half must have wondered what he had let himself in for. For the next decade the brilliant performances turned in by 'King' Charlie made him a legend on Wearside.

Before the dangers of smoking were known football followers were targeted by tobacco companies. Various sets of football cards were given away in packets of cigarettes. In the post-war period the trend of cigarette cards switched to safer products like tea. In 1958 Lambert's of Norwich produced a series which included Sunderland. The badge showed the town's old coat of arms.

ugh tackling Jimmy McNab made his
nderland debut as an eighteen-year-old
inst Ipswich on 20 September 1958. Shortly
er the start of Sunderland's first season in the
cond Division Alan Brown decided to put all
 faith in a policy of youth. He pitched the
mer Scottish Schoolboy international into
 first team along with Len Ashurst and Cecil
vin. All three were to be seasoned veterans
en promotion was eventually achieved.

After impressing scouts from a number of
clubs while playing for St Hilda's School in
Southwick, Jimmy Montgomery signed for his
hometown club in October 1960. He made
his debut a year later against Walsall in the
League Cup while still only seventeen.

Ian Lawther challenges for the ball in the match against Lincoln City at Roker Park (
3 September 1960. At the time Lincoln were bottom of the Second Division with Sunderlar
hoping to mount a promotion challenge. Lawther had been the club's leading goalscorer t
previous season and a goal against Lincoln helped towards him repeating the feat at the end
the 1960-61 campaign. The signing of Brian Clough in the summer of 1961 was to signal t
end of the Northern Ireland international's Roker career.

...nderland's Ambrose Fogarty looks on as the Lincoln 'keeper covers his goal. The game ended ...a 2-2 draw with goals from Lawther and Fogarty. This was Sunderland's first dropped home ...int of the season and they eventually finished in 6th place.

...n Ashurst (left) and Brian Clough had ...ker careers that contrasted sharply. Full ...ck Ashurst made over 400 League ...pearances for the club between 1958 and ...70. Prolific goalscorer Clough played only ... League games but scored 54 goals in his ...ef stay on Wearside. Both men went into ...anagement: Ashurst was Roker boss ...tween 1984 and 1985, while Clough was ...nderland supporters' choice for the post for ...ny years.

ENGLISH CUP - Sixth Round

Sunderland v. TOTTENHAM

AT ROKER PARK GROUND, SUNDERLAND,

ON SATURDAY, MARCH 4th - 1961

At 3-0 p.m.

GROUND   Fulwell End

N⍛ 3052

This Ticket is issued subject to the Rules and Regulations of the F. A. and the F.L. Price of Tickets will not be returnable in any circumstances if the match has to be abandoned or postponed.

PRICE 3/6

A ticket for Tottenham's Sixt Round FA Cup visit on 4 March 1961. Over sixty thousand packed into Roker Park to see if Sunderland could knock Spur off their 'Double' chasing course.

When Willie McPheat scored an equaliser against the Cup favourites at Roker Park some of t ecstatic supporters spilled on to the pitch. Despite having played all over the world Dan Blanchflower had never heard anything like the 'Roker Roar' before. He and the rest of t Spurs team were thankful for the respite the mini invasion brought. It gave them time compose themselves and they managed to withstand the Sunderland onslaught. In the replay White Hart Lane, Spurs stormed into the next round with a 5-0 victory.

...ipper Charlie Hurley is carried shoulder high by team-mates after promotion was assured in ...e last home game of the 1963-64 season. To the relief of the 50,827 crowd a 2-1 win over ...arlton booked a return to the First Division. After the game the players did a lap of honour ...ore returning to the dressing-room. The crowd would not leave and started chanting 'Char-...., Char-lie'. The Sunderland skipper and the rest of the team were forced to come out again.

...fore joining Sunderland in April ...61 George Herd had already played ...r Scotland five times. His transfer ...m Clyde cost the club £42,500. ...he skilful inside forward only missed ...games in the promotion campaign ...oring 13 goals.

Sunderland's line-up at the start of the 1964-65 season. Back row: Cecil Irwin, Martin Harvey, Derek Forster, Jimmy McNab, Len Ashurst. Front row: Brian Usher, George Herd, Nicky Sharkey, Charlie Hurley, Johnny Crossan, George Mulhall.

Fifteen-year-old Derek Forster made history when he played in Sunderland's first game back in the top flight on 22 August 1964. The England Schoolboys 'keeper became the youngest ever First Division player in the game against Leicester City at Roker. After three games the club brought in the experienced Sandy McLaughlan and then the consistency of Jimmy Montgomery, after returning from injury, restricted the young prodigy's progress.

Within days of Ian McColl's appointment as Sunderland manager Jim Baxter was signed for a record £72,500 fee from Rangers. The club had been chasing the stylish Scottish International even before McColl took over. His performances at Ibrox and for the national side had brought 'Slim Jim' to the attention of all the top clubs. On his arrival at Roker he remarked 'This is wonderful. I wouldn't wish to be going to a better club'.

At the time George Kinnell signed for Sunderland in October 1966 he was Oldham's leading goalscorer, however, at Roker he was to make his mark in defence. The Scot made an impressive debut at centre half in a 2-1 victory over Stoke City. This ended a run of 9 League and Cup games without a win. The next game proved how valuable an acquisition Kinnell was when Sunderland recorded a 3-0 win at St James' Park.

Sunderland first team squad for the 1968-69 season. Back row: Geoff Butler, George Mulhall, Martin Harvey, Ian Porterfield, Colin Suggett, Len Ashurst. Middle row: Calvin Palmer, Billy Hughes, Jim Montgomery, Charlie Hurley, Bruce Stuckey. Front row: Bobby Kerr, Gordon Harris, George Kinnell, Colin Todd, Cecil Irwin, George Herd.

One of the greatest post-war Sunderland players was undoubtedly Colin Todd. Born in Chester-le-Street, he was already an outstanding talent when he joined the club as a fifteen-year-old in 1965. By the time he was twenty he was captaining the team in the First Division. In February 1971 Derby County paid £170,000, a record for a defender, for his services. His move to the Baseball Ground brought a belated England call up but 27 full caps was scant reward for this majestic footballer.

...e Sunderland programme for the FA ...p Fourth Round tie against Peterborough ... 18 February 1967. In the previous round ...entford had been beaten 5-2 and a crowd ...almost 44,000 gathered to see if further ...gress could be made against the Posh. ...ey were not to be disappointed: the ...ird Division side were thrashed 7-1. The ...xt round brought three bone-crunching ...mes with Leeds United. The first game at ...ker ended 1-1 with Bobby Kerr suffering ...roken leg after a tackle by Norman ...nter. The scoreline finished the same at ...and Road before a record crowd of ...,892. Sunderland finally went down 2-1 ...a decider at Hull, finishing with only ...e men after George Herd and George ...lhall had been sent off for protesting a ...nalty decision.

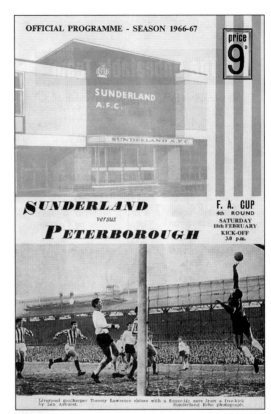

OFFICIAL PROGRAMME - SEASON 1966-67

price 9d

SUNDERLAND A.F.C.

SUNDERLAND A.F.C.

SUNDERLAND

versus

PETERBOROUGH

F. A. CUP
4th ROUND
SATURDAY
18th FEBRUARY
KICK-OFF
3.0 p.m.

Liverpool goalkeeper Tommy Lawrence shines with a finger-tip save from a free-kick by Len Ashurst.
Sunderland Echo photograph.

Hat-trick hero against Peterborough Neil Martin was one of Sunderland's finest post-war centre forwards. Having scored over a hundred goals in Scottish football with Hibernian Martin joined Sunderland in October 1965. By the time he moved on to Coventry City in 1968 he had scored a goal in almost every other game he played for Sunderland. He went on to become one of the few men to have scored a century of League goals in both England and Scotland.

Dave Watson soars above the Orient defence to get a header on goal. Bought from Rotherham for £100,000 in 1970 as a centre forward, he was switched to his original position of centre half and never looked back. After the Cup run brought him to national prominence he won his first England cap against Portugal at the age of 27. He went on to make a total of 65 appearances for his country whilst with five different clubs. After leaving Sunderland he won caps with Manchester City, Werder Bremen, Southampton and Stoke City.

Scottish Under 23 international Dick Malone signed for Sunderland from Ayr in 1970 and quickly became a favourite of the Roker crowd. His surging runs from right back supplemented his defensive prowess. All the newspaper talk before the 1973 Cup Final centred on the havoc Eddie Gray would wreak down the left flank. The Sunderland man silenced his doubters with a performance which forced Leeds to substitute the ineffective Gray. Three years after the Cup triumph he helped Sunderland to promotion to the top flight.

y Hughes was an important factor
he triumphant Cup run in 1973.
icial goals in both games against
nchester City and in the semi-final
wed Sunderland to progress. A
duct of the club's successful youth
em the young Scot's direct style
de him a crowd favourite. Just after
1973 Cup run got underway
ther John the former Celtic
ourite joined him at Roker. An
iry in his first game against Millwall
an end to his Sunderland career. In
'5 Billy Hughes became the last
iderland player to be capped for
otland.

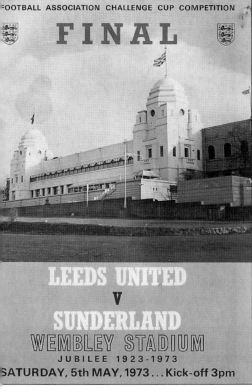

The 1973 FA Cup Final programme celebrating the Jubilee Wembley Final. There was a big difference in price from Sunderland's last Wembley appearance. Inflation had pushed the price from 6d (2½p) in 1937 to 15p in 1973: a six fold increase. Sunderland's ticket allocation had also increased since 1937 doubling to 20,000. However, this still left the Finalists with less than half of the total capacity.

Vic Halom comes away with the ball from Allan Clarke in the Final. Clark was seen as a potential match winner but from th very first tackle Ritchie Pi had his measure. For Leed captain Billy Bremner (le of picture) it was to be another question of so nea yet so far. Although another trophy was denied them they did bounce bac the following season to wi the League.

The signing of Vic Halom from Luton Town for £35,000 in February 1973 was the final piece in Bob Stokoe's jigsaw. The bustling centre forward brought power to an attack that was now capable of scoring against any team in the land. Halom's thunderbolt against Manchester City in the Fifth Round replay was one of the greatest goals ever seen at Roker Park.

e moment that stunned the football
rld: Ian Porterfield hammers home
e goal that brought the FA Cup
ck to Sunderland after a gap of
rty-six years. Unusually it was not
red with the Scot's cultured left
t but with his unfavoured right.

nderland's goal hero could have
en playing on opposite sides in the
73 Cup Final. As a schoolboy he
nt time at Elland Road but was
me sick and he did not return to
rkshire. Leeds' loss was
nderland's gain when he joined the
b from Raith Rovers in 1967.

With Leeds piling on the pressure in search of an equaliser Jimmy Montgomery produced one of the greatest saves ever seen at Wembley. He saved a goalbound Trevor Cherry header but the ball fell to Peter Lorimer. The man with the hardest shot in the game struck it perfectly. Monty flung himself at the ball and somehow managed to parry it away.

Apart from his wonder save at Wembley Monty's performances for the club during the 1960s and '70s make him a candidate for the title of Sunderland's greatest ever goalkeeper. After a spell on loan at Southampton Monty eventually joined Birmingham City in March 1977 after seventeen years at Roker.

The Sunderland skipper on the shoulders of his team-mates proudly holds the Cup aloft. Bobby Kerr had fought his way back from a twice broken leg to lead his side to Cup glory.

The Wembley heroes proudly display the FA Cup. Back row: Arthur Cox (coach), Vic Halom, Dick Malone, Jimmy Montgomery, Ritchie Pitt, Dave Watson, Bob Stokoe (manager). Front row: David Young, Ron Guthrie, Billy Hughes, Bobby Kerr, Dennis Tueart, Ian Porterfield, Mickey Horswill. Like their 1937 counterparts the victorious players received a tremendous welcome on their return to Wearside. The drive from Carrville to Roker Park was cheered by 500,000 people.

CHALFORD
Oral History
SERIES

ROKER PARK
voices

Compiled by
Alan Brett and Andrew Clark

TEMPUS

First published 1997
Copyright © Alan Brett and Andrew Clark, 1997

The Chalford Publishing Company
St Mary's Mill, Chalford,
Stroud, Gloucestershire, GL6 8NX

ISBN 0 7524 1063 6

Typesetting and origination by
The Chalford Publishing Company
Printed in Great Britain by
Bailey Print, Dursley, Gloucestershire

Acknowledgements

Special thanks to Phil Curtis, Peter Gibson and Dave Bowman for supplying
information and photographs.

We would also like to thank:
Tony Affleck, Ian Brunskill, May Cook, Stan Close, Jean Fowler, Phil Hall of
Sunderland Central Library, Peter Martin, Northeast Press, Geoff Pearson, Jeff
Richardson, Bob Robinson, Ian Wright.

Cover photograph by John Yearnshire

Bibliography

Charlie Buchan, *A Lifetime In Football*, Phoenix House 1950
Raich Carter, *A Footballer's Progress*, Sporting Handbooks 1950
Simon Inglis, *Football Grounds of England and Wales*, Collins 1983
Len Shackleton, *Clown Prince of Soccer*, Nicholas Kaye 1955
Penny Watson, *My Dear Watson*, Barker 1981

Contents

Two Sunderland fans celebrate the dawn of a bright new era at the 1976 Durham Miners' Gala after Bob Stokoe's side were promoted from the old Second Division as champions. No one could have foreseen then the Durham coalfield, the bedrock of the club's support for generations, would be obliterated in less than twenty years and that the club would be starting the 1997-98 season in a new stadium on the site of the old Wearmouth Colliery.

Introduction

he feature which elevates Roker Park to the ranks of 'special' is the people who fill it and the
ker Roar which when caught in the sea breeze, is sent swirling across the roof tops.

Simon Inglis
Football Grounds of England and Wales

When Sunderland Association Football Club was established in 1879 its founding fathers had little idea that the team would capture the hearts of thousands of otball supporters. Folk from Wearside and the surrounding area embraced the game d for the next century Sunderland fans became famous for their passion for football.

Football is a favourite topic of conversation and people like to remember great mes, players, away matches, goals or their fellow supporters. This book is made up of e memories of Sunderland fans both young and old. They have had the minimum of liting to maintain the feeling of the tales told by fans. The authors have tried to be ithful to the style of the story teller. This has meant, at times, including local dialect. glossary of some of the terms which may be strange to 'foreigners' is included at the nd. Also included is a list of some of the places, such as pubs, cinemas, schools, etc, hich are mentioned in the text, many of which are now gone. Many of the stories re not just about football and some recall changes not only in Sunderland but in life s well.

The book is not a complete history of Sunderland Football Club but the story of oker as told by supporters. The memories span from just after the First World War to e heartbreaking relegation from the Premiership at Selhurst Park. Some stories have ome from people who live in the shadow of Roker Park while others are from fans ho live on the other side of the world. In some instances we have spoken to several enerations from one family.

Many of the photographs have come from the people who are telling the stories lthough we have included some portraits of players and action from games.

This 'oral history' has a common theme: the loyalty of Sunderland fans to their eam. The unique humour of supporters, essential to get them through the bad times, lso comes across strongly.

Roker Park may now be gone but it will never be forgotten. Many of the stories ecalled in this book will be told time and time again as people share favourite nemories of the Roker Roar.

The authors would like to thank all those who have been kind enough to share their memories with us:

Tariq Ahmed, Tracy Ahmed, Tommy Allen, Billy Barker, Mickey Bute, Margaret Calvert, Elizabeth Clark, Harry Clark, Pauline Clark, Ron Collins, Arthur Curtis (New Zealand), Phil Curtis, Marjorie Curtis, George Forster, Stan Fowler, Irene Gibson, Mark Gibson, Peter Gibson, Ron Gormley, Dave Harrison, Lesley Harrison, Ray Hassan, Alf Henderson, Audrey Henderson, Karen Henderson, Neil Henderson, George Hoare, John Hoban (Australia), Tommy Howey, Davie Howey, Alf Johnson, Karen Johnson, Tommy Keegan, Andrea Lane, Wilf Lathan, David Lathan, Bill Lynch, Dennis Martin, Kathleen Martin, Ronnie McGuire, Terry McIvor, Stephen Morrissey, Andrew Pace (Hong Kong), Joan Pace, Bobby Pearson, Geoff Pearson, Sally Pearson, Bob Robinson, Barry Rodgerson, Hans de Roon, John Ryan, Jack Sanderson, Jimmy Smith, Michael Stephenson, Billy Swan, Mark Taylor, Margaret Tedder, Jackie Turnbull, John Urch, John Yearnshire.

A postcard from the turn of the century.

Billy Bainbridge and son Neil in the colours of the club Billy loved all his life.

CHAPTER 1

Red & White Eyes

*p in the north-east, the crowd takes its football very seriously. They are strongly partisan
ad want their team to win every time. I think they know more about the game than southern
owds. They certainly express their opinions more freely. But they are extremely loyal, good-
earted and have a keen sense of humour.*

harlie Buchan, who starred for Sunderland either side of the First World War.

ae Roker End celebrates a goal in the mid 1980s.

Founding Father

I t would have been about 1918, when I
was eleven-years-old, when 'Daddy'
Grayston came to Stansfield Street as
the Headmaster. Before he arrived we
had no football team at the school but
Mr Grayston was sport mad and he soon
had football and cricket teams going.
He often would remind the boys that it
was schoolteachers who first began
Sunderland Football Club and added
that he was one of them. He always
came and supported our school matches
which were played on a pitch just off
Sea Road. It was on a bank and made
up mostly of clay and stones. There was
no doubt that Mr Grayston certainly
knew his football.

Wilf Lathan

John Grayston left
Halifax in 1877 to
take up a teaching
post at Hendon
Board School. Not
long after James
Allan arrived from
Glasgow
University and it
was he who brought football (as opposed to rugby
football) to the town. They were among those at
a meeting in 1879 at the British Day School in
Norfolk Street that led to the formation of
Sunderland and District Teachers' Association
Football Club. Both men turned out for the side
in the early years. On one occasion a hansom cab
was sent to pick up Grayston and take him to the
Dolly Field in Horatio Street in Roker. He
returned the favour by scoring a hat-trick for
Sunderland – which by then no longer exclusively
comprised teachers.

Jack Lathan and son Wilf. Jack was
Sunderland's first FA Cup Final appearance. H
was part of the vast crowd at Crystal Palace
1913. Wilf was at the club's next appearance
the Final in 1937.

Mind that Child

A fan at the back of the ground
would call to those around him,
'Child coming' and I would be lifted up
and transferred, head over head, to the
bottom of the Fulwell End.

Arthur Curtis

...ll Together

There never used to be segregation for away fans even when we played ...ewcastle. In one derby game I heard a ...out from behind me – 'Dorty Horley' in a proper Geordie accent. A ...ewcastle fan was complaining that ...harlie Hurley was fouling their centre ...rward Barry Thomas. 'Get away man', ...houted back. There was always a bit ...ght-hearted banter between the two ...ts of supporters.

...eorge Forster

...riendly Argument

You would have arguments with the visiting supporters but at the end of the game you would shake hands and say, 'See you next season.'

Marjorie Curtis

Match, Pictures & Supper

My parents had their own routine for match days in the 1920s. They would watch the game then go to the King's Theatre in Crowtree Road to see the first house. On the way home they would buy $\frac{1}{2}$lb of bacon and a 1 lb of parsnips for their supper. They would also go into Jacky White's Market to a secondhand bookshop. My dad would buy a western and my mother a romance. When they got home they would sit reading their books while eating their bacon and parsnips.

Joan Pace

...nderland's squad for the 1920-21 season. After the First World War life in Sunderland began to get ...ck to normal. A match at Roker Park was a popular form of entertainment for thousands of Wearsiders ...this time.

11

Sunderland has always had support in Durham villages like Seaham. The *Seaham Weekly News* of 2 March 1906 advertises a film show of the Sunderland v Aston Villa match which took place a few days before.

Seaham Lads

I started going to Roker Park in the early 1930s with my father. We would get a train called the 'autocar' from Seaham Harbour and get off at Monkwearmouth Station. We then got a tram to Gladstone Street. When the game started he would lift me on to his shoulders so I could see. After a while he would get tired and then put me down on to the terraces. Once I was down I couldn't see and would have to follow the game from the sounds of the crowd. He should have put me in the straw at the edge of the pitch with the other kids. It was a big disappointment not to see what was going on and it put me off football for a long time.

George Forster

Watching in Comfort

At some games, when the ground was packed, the police allowed youngsters on to the edge of the pitch because of the crush. They used straw in those days to protect the pitch in bad weather and it would be piled up at the sides. You could watch the match sitting in this straw.

Peter Gibson

Gym Girls

My sisters Ethel and Florrie took part in a mass gymnastic display at Roker Park in 1935. In the same year I saw my first match. I went along with my dad and sisters. I was about ten-years-old at the time. The following year we went in the newly opened Clock Stand. My sisters stood at the back while I was down the front. I have followed Sunderland ever since. I have been a season ticket holder since 1961.

Billy Barker

anguage Please

My father took me to my first game in 1938 when the visitors were entford. My dad deliberately chose at match because a small crowd was pected. We walked to the match from y home in Brinkburn Street. It seemed me that the whole town was walking the match. Wearmouth Bridge was solutely packed with fans. I recall my sappointment when I realised that aich Carter wasn't playing but this was fset when it was pointed out that rentford had the current Scotland ntre forward, Dave McCulloch, aying. He didn't impress me much d Sunderland won 1-0 through an ldie Burbanks goal. During the match meone began swearing. I remember en around me shouting at the swearer pinting out that there were bairns earby and he immediately apologised. I n't think that anything like that ould happen today. We travelled me on one of the special trams that ere waiting in Roker Baths Road. here were five or six of them lined up d we were home in no time at all. he trams ran on rails and there were traffic jams then.

on Gormley

eturn of the Prodigal

The first match I went to was the first League game after the Second orld War in 1946. I was eleven-years- d and quite small. I was in the Fulwell nd and I could see what was

Ron Gormley is well known for his work for Sunderland Primary Schools football.

happening at the Roker End but not much else apart from when the ball was in the air. When we were on our way to Roker Park we saw Raich Carter standing at the Wheatsheaf talking to a policeman. This was only a couple of hours before the kick-off. He had only left Sunderland the year before to join Derby County but he got a good reception from the crowd when the teams came out. There was no animosity towards him like there is today towards players who leave a club. In those days most animosity was against dirty players.

George Hoare

Hendon Lads

We used to drink in pubs in Hendon Road before matches, just after the Second World War. At the time this was one of the busiest streets in town. There was The Salutation, Queen's Hotel, Hendon Hotel and The Divan and many others in nearby streets. We would then walk up to the town and across Wearmouth Bridge and then on to the ground. We thought nothing of the walk as most people used 'Shanks' Pony' in those days. When we got to Roker Park it cost us a bob to get in.

Tommy Howey

Wrestling at St James'

I used to go to Roker Park one week and St James' Park the next. At Newcastle I used to walk from the station to the ground with former schoolmate Ernie Taylor. He then went in the players' entrance and turned out for United. After the game I would then go to nearby St James' Hall for a night of wrestling.

Billy Barker

Coals to Roker

My first visit to Roker Park was in 1947 when I was nine. I can't remember the opposition. I just remember the huge swell of people, the atmosphere and the goodwill of the crowd. I got the bus from Red House Estate carrying a paper carrier bag of coal. My dad worked at Wearmouth Colliery and we got a ton of the stuff each month for free. I jumped off the bus as it rounded the Wheatsheaf roundabout. The stop should have been the Cora Cinema but we would jump off at the roundabout. I delivered the coal to my teacher who lived in Roker Avenue. It was a fortnightly gift to her, with whom, at nine, I was madly in love. From there I walked, hopped and ran among an ever-growing number of supporters making their way to Roker. The streets in those days were owned by the pedestrians. The few cars would give way to us – the fans. I would go to my aunt's house in Osborne Street, not 50 yards from Roker Park. She would open her back yard and offer to house bicycles at 3d each. My entrance fee would then be earned.

Arthur Curtis

Buses, Ferries & Trams

There were always two bus loads from Easington Lane to Sunderland on matchdays in the 1940s and '50s. When I got into town I would either get a tram to the ground or run down to the East End and catch the ferry for a penny. Even when the crowds were 50,000 or 60,000 you always got into Roker Park. It would only cost you half a crown to get in. The trams were great for getting the crowds away from the ground. They soon got rid of the congestion. For night

The Cora picture house at the Wheatsheaf. Sunderland's new stadium is only a stone's throw from here.

natches I would go straight from the
it. I would get washed in the baths,
ump on the bus and straight to the
natch. I used to be annoyed all
eekend if we got beat. It would really
ffect my temperament. I was
underland daft.

ack Sanderson

Ferry Journey

Just after the First World War my
father used the ferry to get to Roker
Park. We lived in Sans Street South
down the East End and this was the
shortest way to the match.

Margaret Tedder

From the opening of Roker Park until 1957 the ferry from the East End to the Barbary Coast was well used by Sunderland supporters. Its closure meant that East Enders had to travel up to Wearmouth Bridge to cross the Wear.

Out of Towners

A lot of Sunderland supporters come from out of town. There was always a strong contingent from the pit villages of County Durham. There would be coaches from all over the North East parked along the sea front on matchdays.

George Hoare

Packed Like Sardines

I always stood in the Fulwell End behind the goal. I loved it there. If I couldn't get in the Fulwell I would go in the Roker End. At every game you were packed in like sardines. Sometimes during the match you couldn't move except when the whole crowd would move up and down the terraces in a wave. It used to be entertaining every game because it was always attacking play. It's all about winning these days and the managers concentrate on defence. No one really thought about tactics in the 1950s. Even 0-0 draws would be exciting because it was all action.

Alf Henderson

All Together

The crowd would sway in unison as they leaned forward to see corner kicks. It seemed the singing was almost orchestrated by a conductor in the centre of the field.

Arthur Curtis

It Could Have Been Us

When I saw the Hillsborough disaster unfold on TV I thought of the many crushes I'd been in at Roker Park in the past. With the capacity in the last days of Roker Park limited to just over twenty thousand it is hard for some supporters to imagine a crowd three times as big. These massive crowds were at times frightening. You had no control of movement, you had to go with the flow. I learned not to keep my arms at my side as you were even more powerless in that position.

Tommy Allen

Bird's Eye View

Before there was a roof over the Fulwell End there was a wooden fence at the back of the terraces. There was a barrier behind the fence which young lads like me would stand on.

Being a little lad this was the best place we could find to get a good view of the match. You had to get there early because this fence would soon fill up. You got a bird's eye view of the game but you were a long way from the pitch. I think it was too far away to really enjoy the game.

Peter Gibson

Early Finish, Early Start

The first game I went to was with my Uncle Dick in 1960. I was ten-years-old at the time. We left twenty minutes before the end of the game

A couple of Sunderland supporters check on the progress of the building of the roof over the Fulwell End in 1964. The fence at the back was a popular vantage point for youngsters.

Jimmy Montgomery in front of the Roker End. Note the fence at the front of the terrace which was a popular spot for younger fans. Lads would have to get to Roker Park early to find a good place to watch the match.

because he wanted to get away in his car before the crowd came out. I was really sick to leave so early but it didn't put me off. After that I always went on my own. It was only 1/6 when I started going. I would always go very early to get my spot in the Roker End. By 1 o'clock I would be sitting on one of the barriers in the Roker and I wouldn't move until the kick-off. If you got down someone would jump into your place. It used to be agony sometimes to sit so long on the barrier but I was only small so I had to sit somewhere so I could see the pitch. There was no boys' end in those days. Sometimes I would sit on the frame of the floodlight or stand on the fence at the back of the Fulwell

End. I never missed a match until I started playing football myself when I was fifteen. I thought to be a real supporter you had to go to every game. I had a ritual on a Saturday of going to every home match. So if I couldn't go to all the games I stopped going altogether.

Harry Clark

Trip from Alnmouth

In 1961 when I was eleven-years-old I made my first trip to Roker Park. As we lived in Alnmouth in Northumberland it meant two train ourneys so we set off early in the morning. We got in the ground early and found a good position next to the unnel in the Main Stand paddock. I was amazed at the size of the crowd. I was from a small village and had never seen so many people in one place. I remember Charlie Hurley leading the team out and was struck by the size of his legs – they were massive. Another thing that sticks in my mind after all these years was the smell of liniment on the players as they ran out. The sound of the Roker Roar in those days made the hair on the back of your neck stand up. On the long journey home I thought about the match and the stories I would be telling my mates at school. I was different because most people in Alnmouth were Newcastle supporters.

John Yearnshire

The Long Save

I bought my first season ticket in 1962. It was for the Clock Stand and cost £4. I saved the money by collecting national saving stamps. The green ones were 6d and had Princess Anne on them and the blue ones, with Prince Charles on them, were a shilling. It took me ages to save up the full cost.

Dave Harrison

Lucky Gate

I first went to Roker Park in 1960 when I was nine-years-old. I went with a

Local author Peter Gibson and the 'clicky'. This turnstile provided a way for fans to leave Roker Park. Some young supporters also used it to secretly gain entry without paying.

friend of mine. I can't remember who Sunderland were playing but I can remember being very excited. We stood on the fence at the back of the Fulwell End. At half-time I thought I would go to the shop at the corner of Sandringham Terrace, opposite the gates of the Fulwell End, to get some sweets. I had seen some people going out of a turnstile and I assumed if you could get out you could get back in. I said to my friend I was going to the shop but he warned me I wouldn't get back in. But I ignored him and walked down the embankment towards the gate. I went through this big turnstile made of iron bars. It was like a revolving door you see in hotels. I went to the shop and bought some sweets. When I tried to get back into the ground through this turnstile it locked and I was trapped outside. It was designed to allow you out of the ground but not back in. I remember the horror of being locked out. I could see my friend in the Fulwell looking down at me outside the ground and he was just shaking his head. I was wondering how to get back in and I thought I might be able to climb up the gate and squeeze over the top of it. I was only small and I thought I would be able to get through the tight gap at the top of the turnstile. The iron bars of the gate acted like a ladder and I climbed up the gate. I squeezed over the top and went down the other side head first. I was very relieved to be back inside the ground. I went back to my friend who was laughing at me and saying I told you so. After I had discovered this way in to the ground, me and my friends would climb over this gate to get in. It was only two shillings to get in for a boy but that was still a lot of money when pocket money was only a shilling. Money was tight in those days and this was our way of seeing Sunderland play for nothing. We would stand at the shop on the corner and wait until a policeman, who normally stood there, had gone and one at a time we would run from the shop, climb over the gate and into the ground. We called this gate the 'clicky'. We got into most games this way in the early '60s but in one match against Everton in the FA Cup in 1964 there was someone patrolling that gate. This stopped us getting in and we spent most of the match just standing outside the shop. There were lads on the fence in the Fulwell End who shouted the result to us. We knew Sunderland had scored by the roar of the crowd but the lads shouted down who got the goal. Sunderland beat Everton 3-1 that day.

Peter Gibson

Blackburn for Free

The first time I went to Roker Park was in the early '60s and it cost nothing to get in. We had been down the beach and as usual had spent our bus fares on the funfair. As we passed Roker Park the gates were open so it must have been shortly after half-time. I don't remember much of the game but we were playing Blackburn Rovers, who had Ronnie Clayton and Bryan Douglas in their side. Their blue and white halved shirts had V necks almost down to their belly buttons.

Geoff Pearson

Suddick Fans

I lived in Southwick when I was a boy and on a Saturday I would walk round to the shops at Beaumont Street where there would be people queuing up to buy the *Football Echo*. They couldn't wait to get a copy so they could see how Sunderland had got on that day. It shows how important football was to so many people in the area.

Peter Gibson

Master James Lee Finley can't wait to see The Lads in action.

John McIvor in the snow at Hylton Castle in the mid 1980s. He is now a regular in the new stadium.

A last chance to feel the Roker Park turf for young Sunderland supporters. Charlotte, Harry and Rebecca Richardson sport away shirts, while Michaela, in stripes, looks on.

Saturday Specials

As a teenager in the late 1960s me and my friends had a Saturday morning ritual on matchdays. At 9 o'clock we used to go to the Bowling Alley in Newcastle Road where we would spend the morning ten pin bowling. Around midday we emerged into the daylight and headed for the fish shop. On one occasion I remember half a dozen Spurs skinheads with their braces, bovver boots and sheepskins, waiting outside. But there was no trouble, they were just killing time before the match. After a pattie lot we made our way to Roker Park. I'm amazed to recall how early we went to the ground in those days. When the gates opened at 1.00 or 1.30 we went straight in, and we were not alone. Lads in those days made a bee line for the backboards in the Fulwell End. These were a prime viewing site and you had to be early to get your place. For a moment I wondered how we spent the time before kick-off then I remembered we used to spend endless hours on street corners. As I had only known First Division football at the time I did not appreciate the opposition's star players who turned out at Roker every other week. The glamour boys of European Cup winners Manchester United were greeted with derision. George Best was signalled out for mickey-taking treatment with the chant 'Georgie Best' followed by wolf whistles. I only had time for Sunderland. My favourites were Jim Baxter, Neil Martin, Jimmy Montgomery and Colin Todd. Even when we struggled season after season we always had players like these to lift our spirits.

Jackie Turnbull

The Bowling Alley in Newcastle Road was a popular early morning meeting place on matchdays.

Schooldays to Matchdays

When I was at school football played a big part in the lives of me and my friends. We would play football every break-time in the yard at Thornhill School. Often the games would be real thrillers with the results sometimes 25-24. We would start playing straight after our dinner and continue until the bell would ring to get us back into class. My friends and I would also play every Sunday at Barnes Park and as we got older we would play 5-a-side at the Leisure Centre. Football would be our main topic of conversation and we would look forward to every Sunderland game. We always went to the match in a big group. We would meet outside the HMV in High Street and then walk over to Roker Park. I have continued to go with this same group of lads for the past twenty years. During this time we've moved around the ground. We would always stand in the same spot in the Roker End and then we later moved to the Fulwell. We even spent one season watching from the seats. Some of my friends have moved away to work and so there are less of us who go to every game. Even today when we get together we still talk about football. After games I phone friends in Surrey, Birmingham and Hertford to tell them the score and give them a match report.

Stephen Morrissey

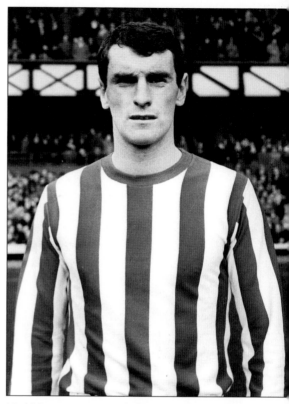

Neil Martin a great Sunderland centre forward of the '60s. The Scottish international scored a century of goals in both English and Scottish football.

Blyth Spirit

Most lads go to the match for the first time with their dads. But my dad played football on a Saturday and so I couldn't go. The first game I went to wasn't a Sunderland match but was at Blyth Spartans. I was about eight at the time. My dad didn't pay for me to get in, he just lifted me over the turnstile. There was quite a big crowd because it was during Blyth's famous Cup run. I enjoyed my first taste of football but my dad said, 'Wait till we go to Roker Park and then you will see a real game and a

What the well dressed Sunderland supporter was wearing in 1978.

big crowd.' My first game at Roker was on Easter Monday against Notts County in 1979. We went in the Roker End. I couldn't believe how many people were there. My dad told me to stand at the front where the kids went while he stood near the back. It was a great game. I couldn't believe the celebrations when we scored. People seemed to be going mad. We scored four times and by the time the last goal went in I was soon joining in with the wild celebrations.

Ronnie McGuire

Hotshot Hawley

I went to my first game at Roker Park in December 1980. It was against Arsenal and Sunderland won with John Hawley scoring a great goal. He shot from well outside of the box and the crowd were buzzing after the goal. I couldn't believe how great the atmosphere was at Roker because it was all new to me. I was overwhelmed by it. I was in the Fulwell End and sat on one of the barriers so I could see. During the game one of the players shot wide and the ball whizzed past me. I fell off the barrier with the shock. After that first game my dad would take me in the Clock Stand so that I could see the game better. Some little lads stood on small boards hanging from ropes from the top of the wall which separated the standing paddock with the seats. It was a good idea but my dad placed me behind an advertising board near the corner flag beside the Fulwell End. At that time I didn't know the rules of the game very well. When we were walking home and talking about the game a little argument would take place over the final score. My dad would say the score was 2-1 but I was convinced it had been 3-2. I used to count the disallowed goals. I didn't know about offside.

Mark Gibson

The Wrong Colours

I couldn't believe the strip Sunderland played in during the early 1980s. The pin stripe shirt was an insult to Sunderland fans. A hundred years of traditional red and white stripes were brushed aside by the designers who came up with a revolting strip. The supporters are proud of the colours their teams wear and they don't like radical

hanges. There was a fuss made in the
960s when the team started wearing
ʰhite shorts. It was fitting that the
lack shorts returned for the season we
ʲon the FA Cup in 1973.

ᵢilly Swan

ᵢcarf Trick

W hen I was eleven I used to go to
Roker Park with some older lads
ᵒm the 'Squares' of Southwick. At one
ᵃme a big lad scaled the wall at the
ᵘlwell End and hoisted the little lads,
ᵢcluding me, up with scarves tied
ᵒgether. The highlight of that game
ʲas at the end when we invaded the
ᵢtch despite warnings from the police.
ʰere was a strong police presence in
ᵗose days.

ᴹark Gibson

ᵢnd of an End

t was a sad day when the Roker End
was partly demolished in the early
ᵗ80s. I had always stood in the Roker
ᵗd regarded it as my home. It didn't
ᵃtter what the weather was like we
ᵒuld always stand on the terrace,
ᵗposed to the elements. While the
ᵒker End was being reduced we stood
ᵗ the Fulwell but it wasn't the same.
ᵗlthough we did enjoy being under
ᵒver, we were glad to be back in our
ᵒt when the Roker was re-opened.

ᵒnnie McGuire

Mark Gibson is all set for his first game at Roker
Park in December 1980.

Autographs and Programmes

M y best early memories are of
standing with about thirty or forty
little lads outside the players' entrance.
We were waiting for the players to get
their autographs. Sometimes I would get
lucky. I would wait outside of Roker
Park at quiet times on afternoons during
the week in the hope of seeing a player.
I was also an avid programme collector.
I had thousands of them. I lived in
Burntland Avenue, Southwick near to
Inkerman Print who produced the
programme at that time. I used to get
into the skip outside their factory to get
the rejects. On one occasion I climbed
into the skip but couldn't get out. My
friends ran for help and two big lads
came and pulled me out.

Mark Gibson

The Roker End was just a pale imitation of its former glory when Roker Park closed in 1997.

Happy Days

There was always a comedian on the terraces. Always someone who would get the crowd laughing. I think football is too serious now.

George Forster

Coaching from the Terraces

In one game Tim Carter was in goal and he seemed to take an eternity to pick up a ball. My mate Ray shouted at the top of his voice, 'Pick it up.' Carter immediately gathered the ball as if responding to Ray's advice. Half the Roker End was laughing at this bit of impromptu coaching.

Ronnie McGuire

Joplings' Dummies

For years there was a guy in the Roker End whose voice could be heard above all others. He was quick to give Sunderland players a tongue-lashing. One of his favourite sayings was, 'You're standing about like Joplings' dummies.'

Tommy Allen

Threepenny Bit Head

If a header went astray somebody in the crowd would shout, 'Threepenny bit head.' They likened him to the multi-sided old coin because it came off his head at all angles.

Mark Taylor

'Threepenny Bit Head' was a cry often heard at Roker Park.

window display at the famous department store John Street showing Sunderland's latest strip. otballers at Roker Park were likened to Joplings' mmies by one supporter.

In the 1960s a roof over the Fulwell End terracing was a big improvement in supporters' comfort. Right up until the end of Roker Park the majority of fans were happy to stand to watch The Lads.

Today seating is the order of the day. Supporters try out seats in the new stadium as it nears completion. The new ground's capacity allows for a return of the big crowds that once packed Roker Park.

CHAPTER 2
Canny Lads

s everyone knows, my playing days with Sunderland didn't last very long. Yet it was ertainly the happiest time I've ever had with a football club.

rian Clough, whose Roker career was tragically cut short by injury.

thur Wright reads his newspaper while receiving the 'steam treatment'. Johnny Mapson & Co look on.

Harry Martin in later life. The Sunderland and England winger played in the 1913 FA Cup Final at Crystal Palace.

Early Days

My dad took me to see my first ever match at Roker Park. It was in 1919 against Aston Villa and the score was 2-1. I can remember Clem Stephenson scoring Villa's goal. I went regularly after that and in the 1920s hardly missed a game. I can still reel off the names of the players from that era: Scott, Hobson, Young, Cuggy, Kasher, Poole, Death, Buchan, Travis, Moore and Martin. Billy Death used to gallop rather than run and Charlie Buchan headed quite a lot of his goals. He could turn a fella inside out. He used to live in Side Cliff Road and often walked to the match with many of the supporters.

Wilf Lathan

The Bank of England Days

If Sunderland were going through a lean spell they would go out and buy star player to generate some interest. Sunderland had money in those days. This was at the time before sponsorship but Sunderland had a lot of money because the gates were always high. Of course, the players weren't paid very much so money would go on transfers.

George Hoare

Sunderland goalkeeper Leslie Scott – st remembered by Wilf Lathan after over seven years.

Wage Control

Money has spoilt football. The maximum wage used to be £10 a week during the playing season, £7 in the close season, £2 if you won and a £1 for a draw.

Marjorie Curtis

Barney's Blockbuster

I can recall Barney Travis busting the net at Roker Park with a shot. It was in a game against Sheffield United and he made contact with the ball at the same time as a defender. The referee had to check the net to make sure it was a goal. Travis had a fruit shop in Jacky White's market and was often in there serving.

Alf Lathan

Thursday Deadline

Sunderland had a great half back line in the 1930s. There was Hastings, Thomston, Clarke, McNab, Wright and Thomson. If you were injured you wouldn't get back into the team until someone else was injured. So everyone was fighting for a place. The team was picked on a Thursday when the directors met at tea-time. If you weren't then you didn't play on the Saturday. There were no late fitness tests just before a game.

Marjorie Curtis

A. HASTINGS

Scottish international Alex Hastings was unlucky to miss the 1937 FA Cup Final appearance through injury.

Alex the Great

I only saw Alex Hastings play wartime football. At that time he was slow and overweight but what a footballer. His left foot was magic. What a player he must have been in his prime.

Jimmy Smith

Raich's Thunderbolt

During the 1942 War Cup Final at Roker Park Raich Carter scored the best goal I've ever seen. I was standing in the Clock Stand close to the half-way line. Carter received the ball with his back to the Fulwell End goal. He was about five yards inside the Wolves half. In one movement he controlled the ball, swivelled and hit the hardest shot I've ever seen. It rocketed into the net. The crowd was silent for a few seconds

A Sunderland forward line from the late 1930s. Left to right: Carter, Bolton and Bett.

hardly believing what they had witnessed before a huge roar greeted the goal.

Ron Gormley

Little Diamonds

When I was a boy I went to Diamond Hall School with Ernie Taylor. Ernie was a brilliant footballer who later played for Sunderland, Newcastle, Blackpool, Manchester United and England. Before his career got off the ground it nearly ended. He had an eye infection and nearly went blind. He had to wear dark glasses for about eighteen months. In the same school team was a lad called Gordon Laverick and Ernie thought Gordon w the better footballer. Gordon played fc Newcastle United Youths but had to stop because he could not afford to los 7/6 for the shift he lost.

Billy Barker

king the Sea Air

lived in Bright Street and often on mornings I saw the trainer Billy illiams running with the players along e sea front to Whitburn. Fans then dn't treat players like gods the way ey do today.

ilf Lathan

oals from Corners

Today they think it's wonderful if a player scores from a corner but in e pre-war days Sunderland had Eddie urbanks, Len Duns and Bert Davis ho could easily score from corners. nd that was with a heavy ball not the resent day light one.

arjorie Curtis

Sunderland winger Len Duns' career spanned the years either side of the Second World War. After playing in the 1937 Cup Final he would have been at his peak when League football was suspended for the war years.

top Gap

After the war Sunderland's buying always seemed to be 'stop gap'. Ken Villingham, an England international efore the war, was signed from luddersfield. He did not play many ames and was allowed to move on. nother was Jack Jones from Everton ho retired after a couple of seasons. Many of the players had seen better days hen they arrived at Roker.

illy Barker

Dream Debut

It's funny how many players come to Sunderland and do very well on their debut. Ronnie Turnbull was bought from Dundee in 1947 and scored four goals in his first game against Portsmouth. He was never so prolific after that.

George Hoare

Fred Hall (right) getting some coaching tips at Roker Park.

Spectacular

In the years before and after the Second World War Sunderland's goalkeeper was Johnny Mapson. His saves at times were spectacular. He was a great 'keeper.

Jack Sanderson

Lefty

Arthur Wright always played with only his left foot. You would think he had only one foot, but what a foot it was. He wasn't as good as Jim Baxter at left half but he wasn't far short.

George Hoare

Durham Lads

I always liked local lads playing for Sunderland. I thought they played for the glory and not for what was going in their pockets. Fred Hall from No Place in Durham was a great stopper. We called him the 'Pigeon Man' because he was a pigeon fancier. Washington's Jack Stelling was another who gave his heart and soul for Sunderland.

John Ryan

A trio of Sunderland strikers in the 1950s. Left to right: Charlie 'Cannonball' Fleming, Len Shackleton and Ted Purdon.

The Clown Prince

Len Shackleton was George Best and Bobby Charlton all rolled into one. He was the first player to start short corners and things like that. He could kick a ball with under spin on it and it would roll back to him. You would think the ball was on elastic his control was so good. But he wasn't a ninety minutes man. He would be brilliant for about half an hour.

Jack Sanderson

Relegation Saviour

When Shackleton was signed by Sunderland in February 1948 he turned the side around. I think the team would have been relegated that season if it wasn't for Shack. He was so clever with brilliant control and balance. He had a good shot but wasn't much of a header of the ball. I think the opposition was frightened of him because they didn't know what he was going to do next.

George Hoare

Corner Trick

Shackleton was so brilliant he occasionally out-thought himself. But I remember seeing him for England against Wales when he was cornered by a Welsh full back. Shack side-footed the ball against the corner post so that it deflected past the defender and left him free to present a perfect left cross.

Arthur Curtis

The Wizard

It was a joy to watch Len Shackleton. No one today can control the ball like he could. He used to make referees mad. Shackleton would stand with his foot on the ball and when the ref came to take it off him he would flick it over the top of the referee's head. He was a wizard with the ball.

Marjorie Curtis

Unsung Hero

Willie Watson was a real gentleman. He hardly ever gave away a foul. He was a class player with real skill. He won four England caps and would have got more but Billy Wright was the regular right half and he was always chosen. I think that is why Wright was never popular at Sunderland. We thought Watson was the better player.

George Hoare

Willie Watson was a lovely footballer – a real gentleman. In derby matches in the 1950s Jimmy Scoular used to kick lumps out of him but he never retaliated.

Kathleen Martin

England cricketer and footballer Willie Watson was one of the most popular Sunderland players of all-time.

...atthews Tamer

...aw Arthur Hudgell play against
...tanley Matthews and the winger
...rdly got a kick. Hudgell played him
...t of the game. Matthews never
...med to give his best away from
...me. He played most of his best games
... Blackpool and Stoke at home.

...orge Hoare

...ewsagent Footballers

...worked as a paper boy for Ken
...Chisholm. He was a forward in the
...50s who had a newsagents in
...rindon with centre forward Ted
...rdon. During the week they would
...ork in the shop but on a Saturday they
...uld be playing for Sunderland in
...nt of crowds of 50,000. In those days
...ayers had to have other jobs outside of
...otball. They didn't get the big wages
...at footballers do today.

...lf Henderson

...harlie's Shop

...harlie Buchan opened a sports shop
...with someone called Lowings. It
...as in Blandford Street. Lowings was a
...cal cricketer and looked after the
...ricket gear while Charlie seemed to
...ainly look after the football side of the
...usiness.

...ilf Lathan

A Christmas advert for Charlie Buchan's shop in
Blandford Street. Many Sunderland players over
the years have opened shops in the town to
supplement their earnings from football.

Hard Man

The hardest tackler I ever saw
playing for Sunderland was Billy
Elliott. He played outside left and later
wing half but he had started out as a full
back.

Alf Johnson

37

Billy Elliott was one of the toughest players I ever saw. He was a left winger but could also play in defence. He was also a judo expert and if he was tripped by a full back while in full flight, he would roll over, get back on his feet and keep on running. In one game against Newcastle he was up against Jimmy Scoular who was also a tough player with a barrel chest and great big thighs. Scoular and Elliott were stuck into each other right from the start and it was getting worse and worse. At one point Scoular tried to chest the ball down only for Elliott to come in with a two-footed challenge, claiming both the ball and the Newcastle player. Then at half-time Scoular tripped-up Elliott as the two players were walking towards the tunnel. But at the end of the game they shook hands. Players in those days didn't whinge about the treatment they got. They just got on with the game.

George Hoare

Young striker Jack Maltby in action at Roker Park. Doing his national service in Germany did not prevent him from turning out for Sunderland.

38

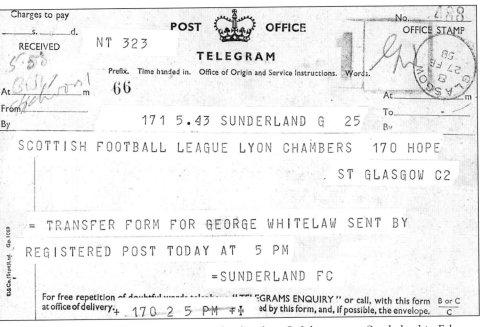

POST OFFICE
TELEGRAM

Charges to pay
___ s. ___ d.
RECEIVED

NT 323

No.

OFFICE STAMP

Prefix. Time handed in. Office of Origin and Service Instructions. Words.

66

At _____ m
From _____
By

171 5.43 SUNDERLAND G   25

At _____ m
To _____
By

SCOTTISH FOOTBALL LEAGUE LYON CHAMBERS   170 HOPE
ST GLASGOW C2

= TRANSFER FORM FOR GEORGE WHITELAW SENT BY
REGISTERED POST TODAY AT 5 PM
=SUNDERLAND FC

For free repetition of doubtful words .... " TELEGRAMS ENQUIRY " or call, with this form   B or C
at office of delivery. 170 2 5 PM   ed by this form, and, if possible, the envelope.   C

telegram confirming the transfer of George Whitelaw from St Johnstone to Sunderland in February 58.

Talent Spotting

Sunderland often played friendly matches against Scottish clubs in the 1950s to check out players they wanted to sign. Charlie Fleming was bought from East Fife after they played at Roker Park in a floodlit friendly.

George Hoare

Special Air Service

Sunderland manager Alan Brown thought so much of Jack Maltby he used to fly him over from Germany for games. At the time the young striker was doing his national service on the Rhine.

Billy Barker

Big Scoring

I once saw George Whitelaw score six goals for the Reserves at Roker. But this was nothing special in the 1950s. Sunderland Reserves used to hammer some teams by scores like 13-1. I think Whitelaw only played a handful of games for the first team.

Phil Curtis

Schoolboy Heroes

Four Sunderland players came to St Hilda's School when I was about ten-years-old. Jimmy Montgomery was one of them. He was a former St Hilda's schoolboy. Charlie Hurley was another player who came. The players were sitting at some tables in the playground

39

One of Sunderland's finest ambassadors, Charlie Hurley (third from left) welcomes visitors to Roker Park during the 1966 World Cup. Charlie also attended countless local events and functions. St Hilda's School at Southwick was one of those who will never forget his visit.

and the whole school queued up to get their autographs. I had a little notebook that I stuck a photograph of Hurley inside which he signed. At the time I was overawed to meet these footballers. In fact a lot of us kids were in awe of them. We all wanted to be footballers at that time and we were at a very impressionable age. King Charlie Hurley was a mountain of a man. The kids at St Hilda's thought he was really special.

Peter Gibson

King Charlie

When Charlie Hurley was playing and we got a corner you knew it would be a goal. When he ran up from defence the crowd would start to chant, 'Charlie, Charlie.' He nearly always won the ball in the air for someone like little Nicky Sharkey to score.

Alf Henderson

No Mean Cricketer

Sunderland football team played Wearmouth Cricket Club at the Barley Hill ground in the early 1960s. It was an annual event that Sunderland provided a cricket team to play the winners of the Durham Senior League. That year Wearmouth had won the league. There was quite a big crowd for the match. Charlie Hurley scored a century. He was a hero anyway and to make a century made him seem even more special.

Peter Gibson

Characters

Charlie Hurley was once led a merry dance by Aston Villa's centre forward Derek Dougan. Hurley was dragged all over the park. I saw Dougan play several times. He was a real character with his fancy haircuts, including a Mohican. There's not enough characters in the game today.

George Forster

The Doog Remembered

My son, John worked with Derek Dougan in Wolverhampton. One weekend John said he was going home to Sunderland and Dougan said he would get him tickets for the game that Saturday. My son didn't believe him because he knew Dougan was a smooth talker. But he did get them and the tickets were left at Roker Park. Denis Smith was Sunderland's manager at that time and he wrote a little note which he put in an envelope with the tickets. It said, 'These are for all the times I kicked him (Dougan).'

Marjorie Curtis

Hat-trick Not Good Enough

John Goodchild made his one and only appearance of the season against Leeds at Elland Road in February 1961. Sunderland won 4-2 and Goodchild scored a hat-trick with all three of his goals coming from shots outside the penalty area. Goodchild never played for Sunderland again.

Mickey Bute

Stan the Man

The best Sunderland player I ever saw was Stan Anderson. He won a place in a team of big money signings when only eighteen. During one game Sunderland were awarded a penalty and nobody wanted to take it. The teenager did not hide and stepped up and took the responsibility.

Billy Barker

Horden-born Stan Anderson spanned the transition from the 'Bank of England' days to Alan Brown rebuilding of the late 1950s and early '60s.

Goalscorer Supreme

Brian Clough was my hero. He was the idol of many Sunderland supporters. He was a goal machine with very muscular legs. It was a disaster when he got injured on Boxing Day in 1962 against Bury. It was the injury which finished his career. He had scored 28 goals in the season up till then and Sunderland had been unbeaten at home. His injury was a disaster and cost Sunderland promotion that season. He did return to play a few games in the First Division which was his ambition but then he moved into management. Sunderland missed a great opportunity by never giving him the Sunderland manager's job. Imagine the success we would have achieved with him in charge.

Peter Gibson

Farewell to Clough

I only saw Brian Clough play once and that was in his testimonial. Over thirty thousand turned out to repay the legendary goalscorer. I remember I took saveloy dips with me for half-time. Clough scored two goals in the 6-2 defeat at the hands of a Newcastle XI.

Tommy Allen

Cecil Special

One of the best goals I have ever seen was scored by Cecil Irwin. Instead of full back he was playing right half for the Reserves when he cracked home a thunderbolt from the halfway line.

Geoff Pearson

Scottish Lads

In the 1960s Sunderland had a lot of Scottish players who formed a clique. The older players such as Jim Baxter and George Kinnell would often be seen in the La Strada nightclub. The younger Scots, such as Bobby Kerr, would be seen at the Bowling Alley in Newcastle Road.

Mickey Bute

Great Debut

Jim Baxter was the best Sunderland footballer I have ever seen. I remember his home League debut in August 1965. He sprayed the ball all over the park against Sheffield United. At times he thought too far ahead of his team-mates. He put balls through that they never read. He scored two great goals in the 4-1 win over Sheffield.

Margaret Calvert

Jim Jim

Jim Baxter was a class player. I thought he was brilliant. I saw him on his debut when he scored two goals. His ball control was out of this world and he was cool with it. There is no substitute for class.

Alf Henderson

Scottish international Jim Baxter, without doubt one of the greatest players of his generation.

Pure Class

I saw Jim Baxter play at Roker Park before he signed for Sunderland. The English League played the Scottish League at Roker in 1964. It was a great game with the outstanding player being Jim Baxter. I think, apart from George Best, he was the best player I ever saw. Sunderland signed Baxter a year later but he had suffered a bad injury and I don't think he was the same player. I think I saw the best of him that night.

Harry Clark

George Kinnell after a hard training session. The tough Scot used to look after his cousin and teammate Jim Baxter.

The Minder

George Kinnell was Jim Baxter's cousin and the rugged defender used to look after Slim Jim. In a match against Fulham at Roker in 1967, Baxter was the target for special treatment and in the end retaliated. There was a melee with the Sunderland man on the ground. Kinnell ran the length of the field to chin Allan Clarke. After things had quietened down the ref sent off

Baxter and a Fulham player. Kinnell and Clarke, who later played for Leeds and England, remained on the field.

Geoff Pearson

TV Horror

I hate watching programmes about George Best on television. They never fail to show him in a game against Sunderland at Old Trafford. The

nderland players, in their light blue
ange strip, are seen being torn apart
the United winger. Even the brilliant
lin Todd was run ragged by the Irish
nius.

mmy Allen

n the Beach

eorge Mulhall often joined me and
my friends for a game of football on
e beach at Roker near the Cat and
g Steps. One time Neil Martin was
sking on the prom with his wife and
asked him to join the game. He
mply stood up and shook his head as
pointed to his legs and said, 'Fifty
ousand pounds these.'

ickey Bute

lash of Styles

teve Whitworth was a good full
back. He would jockey the opposing
nger and keep them tight up against
e touch line. He would never dive in.
n the other wing Joe Bolton would
ve in and if he won the ball would
art chasing up to the other end of the
tch. But if he lost the ball the
pposition would just knock the ball
to the space he had just left.

ave Harrison

Steve Whitworth in England colours. Before
coming to Roker Park in 1978 he won seven
international caps.

Shortest Route

Joe Bolton was hard as nails. In one
game against Burnley in the Cup in
1979 Joe had to contend with a tricky
winger. On one occasion the Burnley
man went down after a challenge and
Joe had to get back in position. Instead
of running around the winger he took
the shortest route and trampled straight
over him. The player jumped up and ran
to the referee to protest but was told to
get on with the game. He just ran over
him. Amazing!

Mark Taylor

45

Roker Roar at St James'

You can understand why Gary Rowell is still such a favourite with Sunderland fans. I think the highlight of his career was the derby match at St James' Park in 1979 when Sunderland won 4-1 and Rowell got a hat-trick. I got into the game late. We heard a loud roar outside the ground and thought we were getting beat. But it was the Sunderland fans who were making all the noise because we had gone into the lead. Once inside we enjoyed every minute of the game. It was the greatest match I ever saw.

Michael Stephenson

Forgetting the Score

When Sunderland signed Stan Cummins in 1979 me and all my friends at school were excited that we had signed a great player. Jack Charlton who was Stan's manager at Middlesbrough, said he would be the first million pound player in English football. That title went to Trevor Francis but we thought Sunderland had made a great signing. When Stan got the ball there always seemed to be a buzz going round Roker Park. When Burnley were beaten 5-0 at Roker, Stan scored four goals. Me and my friends le

The Sunderland squad for the 1982-83 season. Back row, left to right: Pickering, Chisholm, Hindmarch, Prudhoe, Turner, West, Elliott, Atkins. Middle row: Durban (manager), Rowell, Walker, Munro, Procto James, Robson. Front row: Cooke, Bracewell, Venison, Atkinson.

e ground thinking it was 6-0. With all
ese goals flying in we had lost count.
e were only ten-years-old at the time.

lly Swan

V Star

yne Tees television used to show a
football programme on a Friday
ening and it always started with a free
ck from Kevin Arnott. It was a curler
at went over the wall and into the top
rner. Arnott was a class player. He
ice scored a great goal against
anchester United. It won 'Goal of the
onth' on Tyne Tees' *Shoot* programme.

nnie McGuire

eeping Them Out

hris Turner is one of my favourite
players of all-time. I think his best
me for Sunderland was against
ottenham in the Milk Cup at Roker.
e saved everything that night. I think
irner's great form was the main reason
e got to the Final that year. Two
asons before Sunderland went six
imes in a row without conceding a
al. Turner was in goal and Gordon
hisholm and Ian Atkins were in
efence.

ariq Ahmed

Powerhouse

When Sunderland signed Marco
Gabbiadini I wondered what he
would be like. I imagined he would be a
tall, lean Italian type. When I saw him
make his home debut I was first
surprised by his appearance and then
stunned by his performance. Although
he wasn't tall he had the biggest thighs
I've ever seen. From his first touch, I
thought he was brilliant. He had
electrifying pace and power. I knew
straight away he was something special.
Standing in the Roker End it used to
annoy me when blokes would criticise
Marco. Without him we would not have
got out of the Third Division at the first
attempt.

Mark Taylor

The Don

The fans at Roker like to cheer a
hero and Don Goodman fitted the
bill. He never quite achieved the
success he deserved but he could
sometimes change a game. He destroyed
Millwall single-handedly in 1992. The
game was fairly even until the Don took
over. In a few minutes it went from
being an even game to being 6-2 with
Goodman scoring a hat-trick. Millwall
were shell shocked and Sunderland were
running riot with Don at the heart of it.
You could see he was enjoying himself
and was always looking to score again.

Billy Swan

Marco Gabbiadini in action. The striker was an immediate hit with Sunderland fans after signing fro York City for a bargain fee in 1987 and many thought he would go on to become an England player. Th closest he got to international recognition was to turn out for an England 'B' game against Czechoslovak at Roker Park in April 1990. His impressive performance that night did not lead to a full cap but it d confirm his outstanding promise. A year later he was sold to Crystal Palace for a record fee for Sunderland player. Although Marco's career failed to take off after leaving Roker he is still remembere by Sunderland fans as one of the great players to grace the old stadium.

CHAPTER 3
The Roker Roar

Nothing I have ever heard equalled the intensity of that wild roar at Roker Park last week when Sunderland drew level with Tottenham in the sixth round.

Danny Blanchflower, after a Cup tie at Roker in 1961.

One of Sunderland's greatest goalkeepers, Johnny Mapson in action at Roker Park.

Carried to the Match

I went to the record crowd against Derby with a sprained ankle. Two of the Sunderland players carried me up the stairs of the Main Stand so I could watch the game.

Marjorie Curtis

Shut Out

When Sunderland were playing Derby in 1933 I took the day off work to go to the match. But I found that I couldn't get into Roker Park so I went to the Havelock Cinema instead. During the film the score was flashed on to the screen.

Wilf Lathan

Worn Out

When Sunderland beat Derby 6-1 in 1950, I was standing next to a man who told me he had been in the biggest ever crowd at Roker Park in 1933. He said he used to go to the match on his bike which he would leave at a house near the ground. The crush of the crowd was so great that he felt drained when he left the game. When he collected his bike he didn't have the strength to lift his leg over the saddle. So he had to walk home leaning on his bike, he was so worn out.

George Hoare

The scene during Sunderland's record-breaking Cup tie against Derby County in 1933. The crowd of 75,118 at Roker saw Sunderland lose 1-0 to a late goal from the visitors.

The tragic Jimmy Thorpe who died a few days after rough treatment in the game with Chelsea in February 1936.

Gasp from the Crowd

I was at the game against Chelsea when Sunderland's goalkeeper Jimmy Thorpe was kicked in the head. A few days later he died in hospital. His place was taken by Johnny Mapson who looked a lot like Thorpe with his fair hair swept back. When Mapson played his first game for Sunderland there was a gasp from the crowd when he walked on to the field because he looked so much like Thorpe.

Marjorie Curtis

Knockout Goal

The two leg Cup tie after the Second World War against Birmingham sticks in my mind. Sunderland had three of the '37 Cup Final team; Mapson, Duns and Burbanks. Duns headed the winner at Roker Park from a Burbanks cross. Everyone was amazed because Duns just couldn't head a ball. It was a very wet day and the ball was so heavy Duns knocked himself clean out. The Roker End was closed because they had materials stored under the stand. We were passed down to the front and then ran across into the Roker End. By

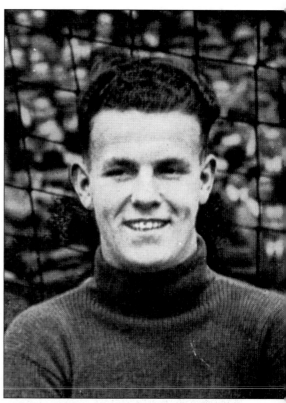

Johnny Mapson bore a striking resemblance to Jimmy Thorpe the man he replaced in the Sunderland goal.

the end of the game there was about 200 kids and a fat policeman in the Roker.

David Lathan

Stung by a Bee

In 1948 against Huddersfield their goalkeeper Bob Hesford had to go off in the first few minutes with a broken leg after he collided with Frankie Bee. Bee was Sunderland's reserve centre forward who didn't make the grade. I couldn't believe Bee could injure anybody because he looked so skinny and weak, he was like a bean pole.

Jack Sanderson

Arsenal Hammered

In one week in 1953 Sunderland bought Jimmy Cowan, Ray Daniel and Billy Elliott all for big fees. The press in the south went to town with Sunderland because the club had bought these players for a lot of money and the team never won any honours. One of the few games that these players did hit it off was against Arsenal when Sunderland won 7-1.

George Hoare

Shadowlands

It was amazing watching the first games played under floodlights in the

1950s. There were parts of the ground in shadow because the floodlights weren't as good as they are today.

Marjorie Curtis

Preston Home & Away

I was at Deepdale for Sunderland's Cup tie against Preston in January 1955. It was one of the best games I've ever seen. Despite the muddy conditions the sides produced a classic. Goals from Purdon and Chisholm gave Sunderland the lead at the interval but Preston stormed back in the second half. The match ended in a 3-3 draw with Sunderland's other goal coming from the brilliant Shack. The replay at Roker a few days later was a big disappointment but Sunderland still won. Without the injured Tom Finney Preston fell to two Chisholm goals.

Jimmy Smith

Quick 'Un

The fastest goal I ever saw at Roker was against Leeds United on Boxing Day 1957 when Sunderland won 2-1. From the kick-off the ball went high to the right wing for Billy Bingham to head it between two defenders and run down the wing. He crossed it to Don Revie who put it into the net. A goal within 20 seconds.

Mickey Bute

Supporters queue at Roker for tickets for the replay against Preston in the 1955 FA Cup. Despite being played on a Wednesday afternoon there was a huge crowd with 10,000 locked out. Secretary George Crow defended the decision to close the gates on safety grounds. He said, 'Yesterday's 57,432 spectators saw the game in comfort.'

Taking on the Best

The early 1960s were a special time for me. Sunderland had a good side at that time and gave some of the top teams in the country hard games. There was a real buzz around the town when Sunderland were going for promotion and taking on the likes of Manchester United, Tottenham Hotspur and Everton in the Cup.

Peter Gibson

Spurs Rattled

Spurs had a great side when they played Sunderland in the FA Cup at Roker Park in 1961. They were a class above Sunderland and went into a 1-0 lead. Dave Mackay was looking very dangerous running down the left to join in the attack. Then a run by Mackay was blocked by Willie McPheat and it looked like the Spurs player had hit a brick wall. That stopped his attacks and Sunderland started to come back into the game. In the second half McPheat

53

scored after a scramble in the box. You can't really explain what happened next. The crowd surged on to the pitch but it wasn't a deliberate act. The Roker End was packed and everyone surged forward. Then all of a sudden people were spilling on to the pitch. Then exuberance took over and there were fans dancing around the pitch. Pitch invasions were unheard of in those days. The crowd had rattled Spurs and Danny Blanchflower's face was as white as his shirt. Every time Sunderland attacked, the Spurs' goalkeeper, Brown, looked over his shoulder to see if anyone was coming on to the pitch. We could have won the game but Dillon, the outside left, miss-kicked when he was clean through. The game ended 1-1 and Sunderland were well beaten in the replay.

George Hoare

Roaring Them On

I was shouting that much in the Cup game against Spurs in 1961 I couldn't talk for a week afterwards.

Dennis Martin

A Man Short

In December 1961 against Walsall, Sunderland played for most of the game with ten men. Stan Anderson was carried off after less than five minutes with a broken cheek bone. Substitutes were not allowed in those days but Sunderland still won the match 3-0.

Mickey Bute

Young supporters run on the pitch to celebrate Willie McPheat's goal against Tottenham in 1961.

The line-ups from the Manchester United programme for Sunderland's visit to Old Trafford in the FA Cup in 1964. Charlton, Best and Law look a frightening forward line even on paper.

Steaming in the Roker End

When we played Newcastle in the 1961-62 season the rain was lashing down at Roker Park. I was in the Fulwell End and you could see the steam rising off the crowd in the Roker End. We won 3-0.

Dave Harrison

The Match You Couldn't Miss

It seemed like everybody in Sunderland thought they had to go to the Cup game against Manchester United in 1964. I went straight to the match from work wearing a rosette made from the lining of a jacket. You couldn't get on the buses because they were so packed so we walked from Pallion. Me and my friend went early to get a place but couldn't even get to the gates the crowd was so great. It was absolute madness. There wasn't any queues and the streets were just solid with people. It was frightening and people started to panic. The police couldn't control the crowds and more and more people were still coming to the ground. I decided not to try to get into Roker and tried to make my way from the ground. A man lifted me on to a parked car. I walked along the roofs of parked cars and used them as a pathway out of the crowds. The cars were all dinted but it was the only way to escape. I lost a shoe that night.

Audrey Henderson

I worked at Doxford's shipyard and got away early for the Man United game in 1964. When we got to the ground it was packed and difficult to move. But when I got inside there seemed to be a lot of room where I was standing in the Fulwell End. I had a good view.

Alf Henderson

I'll never forget that game against Manchester United as long as I'll live. The queues were so bad that even some of the gatemen couldn't get to Roker Park.

George Forster

My father dropped me off in Fulwell Road by Redby School before the Man Utd game. I walked down towards Roker Park and when I turned a corner all I saw was this mass of humanity. There were people everywhere. I got to the ground but couldn't see anyway to get in because the crowd was so packed.

I had a ticket for the Clock Stand but couldn't get near to the gates. So I tried to get in at the Roker End but still couldn't get to the gates. Then someone came past me pushing a wheelchair and people were letting these fans through. So I followed them and got through the crowd and to the Clock Stand. I got in about 7.10 after being dropped off at 5.30. My mam was panicking because she had heard about all the chaos on TV and the radio.

Dave Harrison

When I got inside all us kids were lifted up and passed over the heads of the crowd and down to the front. I watched the game lying down on the running track. Some Manchester United supporters asked me if there was a boys' end because they said that's where we should have been.

Harry Clark

I didn't get into the ground until the last few minutes when the gates were opened near the end of the match. I stood on the corrugated iron roof of the toilets in the Fulwell End. I couldn't see the goals but I saw any action down the wing. There was no way we could get a better view because you could not get on to the terraces they were so packed. But it was great to be part of that exciting game. The atmosphere was tremendous but you took that for granted in those days.

Peter Gibson

We scored first. Then Montgomery took a goal-kick which went straight to Denis Law who scored the equaliser. The man next to me started to cry. He just couldn't believe it. It then went to extra-time. From the kick-off Nicky Sharkey went straight down to their end and set up a goal to put us back in the lead. Everyone in the crowd just went berserk. We thought we had won but near the end a cross came in and it just caught Bobby Charlton's head and it went in. The bloke next to me was now on his knees.

Alf Henderson

Even when the ground was full not everyone went home. Many people who couldn't get in stayed outside and tried to follow the game by the roar of the crowd.

Audrey Henderson

The atmosphere was tremendous. I had been to a lot of games but none were as special as that. It was frightening to be in such a big crowd but everyone was well behaved.

Alf Henderson

When I got out of Roker Park after the game I found one of my shoes had no sole on it. It had been ripped off in the sheer crush.

Bobby Pearson

My husband was a policeman on duty that night. When he got

The morning after the night a hundred thousand people descended on Roker Park to try and see the Manchester United replay.

home he hardly had a button left on his tunic and he had lost his shoe laces.

Marjorie Curtis

I lived in Roker Baths Road near the ground. I couldn't believe the scenes outside our front windows for the Manchester United game in 1964. People were in our garden climbing up the bay windows to get out of the crush. The following morning there were piles of shoes scattered all over the streets with people searching through trying to find their own.

John Urch

The scenes of devastation at Roker Park after the night of mayhem against Manchester United in the Cup in 1964.

Replay Sickness

I went to the second replay against Manchester United at Huddersfield on a Monday night. I had to play the wag from school. It was 0-0 at half-time but by the end of the game we were hammered 5-1. When I got into school the next day I handed in my 'sick' note to the teacher who said, 'Was it a good game?'

Dave Harrison

Lap of Honour

Getting beat off Manchester United in 1964 was disappointing but at least we won promotion at the end of that season. The team did a lap of honour after the last game of the season against Charlton. George Herd was doing handsprings on the pitch. The players carried Charlie Hurley around Roker Park on their shoulders.

Harry Clark

Over the Heads

When I was about 13 or 14 I went with my dad to see Manchester United at Roker. It was not the famous Cup tie of 1964 but as usual there was a massive crowd to see United. We were in the Roker End and people continued to cram into the area we were in. Eventually me and other lads were passed over heads on to the dirt track. I nearly had my head knocked off by a wayward Bobby Charlton shot. I was near the corner flag at the time!

Geoff Pearson

Celtic Invasion

I was ten-years-old when I saw my first Sunderland match. This would have happened the year before in 1964 if it had not been for the huge crowd for the Manchester United Cup game. My mother feared for my safety so when she did allow me to go to Roker Park it was for a friendly – against Celtic! I was in the middle of the Roker End with a friend on a big concrete crash barrier surrounded by Scotsmen. I say men, because that is all I seem to remember, I don't recall anyone near my age there. The Celtic invasion of Sunderland in August 1965 has gone down in legend. Since that time I have been told stories of how they descended on every club and pub in Sunderland and the surrounding estates. Drinking premises dry and sending committee men out for fresh lots! But being so young I only saw what happened around me and that was an experience. A couple of yards from us a Celtic supporter in his thirties held up a five pound note and offered to bet anyone his team would score first. Luckily, there were no takers as Celtic not only scored first but continued to find the net all afternoon. A drunken man in his fifties was drinking from a half bottle of whisky. He got in an argument with a fellow Scot and was head-butted and his eye swelled up like something out of a cartoon. The deliverer of the 'Glasgow Handshake' felt immediate remorse and hugged his victim with both men in tears. I don't recall any of the match itself but Celtic won 5-0. I did not mention any of the trouble to my mother because I wanted to go back to Roker Park for more. The

Charlie Hurley, one of Sunderland's all-time favourites.

following week I saw Sparta Rotterdam play but it wasn't quite the same without the Scots.

Jackie Turnbull

When Celtic visited Roker Park in 1965 I was in the Roker End with a number of friends. It seemed that most of the end was full of Glaswegians. Sunderland were trounced 5-0 and at the end of the game the Roker End was absolutely covered with empty beer and whisky bottles. There were hundreds of them. At that time we were all hard-up schoolboys and as most of the bottles had a return refund of threepence on them it was suggested that we collect as many of the empty beer bottles as we could and return them to the local pub

Sunderland line up before the friendly against Celtic in 1965. Back row, left to right: Martin Harve[...] Charlie Hurley, Len Ashurst, Sandy McLaughlan, Jimmy McNab, John Parke. Front row: Mike Hellawel[...] Harry Hood, Nicky Sharkey, Jim Baxter, George Mulhall.

for the money. As I lived very close to the ground we left as many bottles as we could in my backyard and returned to the ground with large boxes and carriers and proceeded to fill them with the bottles. The backyard was packed with them. Later we went down to The Wolseley and I think we got well over £3 for them. When my mother found out she went mad.

Phil Curtis

Choirboys

The day after the Celtic game we saw some Scottish fans in church. There they were on the Sunday morning still wearing the green and white scarves.

Who knows where they slept on the Saturday night?

Stan Fowler

The Return of the Scots

The local pubs were packed with Scottish fans when Rangers came t[...] Roker for Gary Bennett's testimonial in August 1993. The Red Lion in Roker Avenue did a roaring trade but the takings were down on what they shoul[...] have been. They then realised that the[...] had been changing Scottish pound notes as £5 notes.

Davie Howey

Mixed Dialects

Against Newcastle in 1967 I was near a group of supporters who had Tyneside accents. Some were Sunderland fans while others were Newcastle supporters. They were probably a group of friends who travelled from Tyneside together to watch the game. In those days, even in derby matches, home and away fans mixed together. Albert Bennett was playing for Newcastle. He had a teddy boy hairstyle, all greased back.

Peter Gibson

Gorilla in the Net

In the 1967 derby game at Roker, Sunderland were winning 3-1 and Newcastle came back to snatch a draw. Their centre half John McNamee scored the equaliser in the last minute from a corner. He ended up in the goal and was hanging on the net like a great big gorilla.

Bill Lynch

Tickets for Leeds

My son queued all night for tickets for the Cup tie with Leeds in 1967. In the morning he fell ill and had to come home without tickets. I then went down to the ground and straight away got two tickets.

Billy Pearson

All Red

What was unusual about the Cup game against Leeds at Roker in 1967 was that Sunderland played in their all red shirts and shorts even though they were at home. I was in the Fulwell End and I couldn't see Norman Hunter's tackle that broke Bobby Kerr's leg. I remember Kerr's debut earlier in the season when he scored the winner against Manchester City.

Geoff Pearson

In a Fog

Sunderland played Halifax in the League Cup in the 1967-68 season and Roker Park was shrouded in thick fog. I was in the Roker End and it was so foggy you couldn't see past the half-way line. Sunderland went into a 3-0 lead but all the goals were at the Fulwell End and I didn't see a thing. When the teams swapped ends for the second half Halifax scored twice at the Fulwell. The final score was 3-2 but I came away from that match without seeing a single goal. It could have been 0-0 as far as I was concerned.

Dave Harrison

Hyper-Inflation

When Sunderland played Vasas Budapest in the European Cup Winners Cup in 1973 admission prices were doubled. Having paid the 100%

increase we were hit by another bombshell inside. The cry of the peanut seller sounded different, instead of 5p a bag they cost 10p. When asked the reason for the dramatic rise he replied, 'Well tickets for the match cost twice as much and so ...'

Tommy Allen

Quick Exit

The season after Sunderland won the FA Cup in 1973 everyone expected another good Cup run but they were beaten at the first hurdle against Carlisle. There were power cuts at the time and Sunderland had to play on the afternoon during the week. I took the afternoon off from Thompson's shipyard to go to the game.

Peter Gibson

Card Tricks

In the 1979-80 season Sunderland were unbeaten all season at Roker. We were going for promotion and some of the games were very tense. Against Wrexham we were losing 1-0 for most of the game until Kevin Arnott scored near the end to equalise. The Roker End went wild. The man next to me had a pack of cards in his pocket and during the celebrations they fell out on to the terrace. He picked them up and threw them into the air sending cards flying over people's heads.

Stephen Morrissey

When Sunderland played in their all red shirts for the game at Roker against Leeds in 1967 it was not the first time an unusual strip change had been made in the competition. In a replay at Nottingham Forest in 1930 (left) the referee made Sunderland change at the last minute. They had to borrow Forest change shirts with a red V.

The Last Massive Crowd

had only been to a couple of Sunderland games but when we played West Ham at the end of the 1979-80 season I knew I couldn't miss that match. It was the final game of the season and we had to beat the Hammers to win promotion to the First Division. It was made an even bigger occasion because West Ham had just won the FA Cup a few days before. There was over 47,000 people in Roker Park but it didn't seem too packed. Of course the Roker End was a lot bigger in those days. I have never seen such a big crowd and it will not be beaten unless they build extra stands at our new stadium. The game was played on a Monday night and all day at school me and my friends could talk about nothing else. The match was one of those rare occasions when Sunderland, in front of a big crowd, didn't let down their fans. But me and my friends always knew we were going to win. Goals from Stan Cummins and Kevin Arnott saw us through to the First Division. It was the first game I had gone to with my friends and not with my dad. After that I hardly missed a game.

Ronnie McGuire

Brought Down To Earth

Sunderland had a great start to the 1980-81 season after they had won promotion to the First Division. In the first game of the season we beat Everton and then hammered Manchester City 4-0 away when John Hawley scored a hat-trick. For the next game against Southampton there was a massive crowd. There was a lot of pushing and shoving to get in and I thought the gates would be shut with us locked out. It wasn't just Sunderland's good start to the season which had drawn the crowd to Roker. In the Southampton line-up was Kevin Keegan. He had just returned to English football that season and had surprised a lot of people by signing for Southampton rather than one of the big clubs. He was England captain at the time and had twice won the European Footballer of the Year award. When the Southampton team ran out on to the Roker Park pitch they got a standing ovation. I was really surprised at the time but it was in recognition of Keegan who was probably the best footballer in England at the time. In later years Keegan wouldn't get the same reaction at Roker when he was manager of Newcastle. The Southampton game was a real let down. Sunderland lost 2-1 and our brief stay at the top of the League came to an end.

Billy Swan

Walker Magic

We've always had thrilling games against Manchester United but one of the greatest that I saw was in 1984 at Roker. United had some great players like Mark Hughes, Bryan Robson and Gordon Strachan but Sunderland matched them that day. Robson put Man United in front and

A sight that will never be seen again – Supporters on the terraces in the Roker End against Everton 3 May 1997.

then Hughes made it two. Then straight from the kick-off Clive Walker scored and the come back had started. Then Hughes and Dave Hodgson were sent off and now Sunderland came storming back. First Gary Bennett and then Stan Cummins were brought down and Walker converted a couple of penalties to clinch a hat-trick and put Sunderland into the lead. This all seemed to happen in a few minutes and the atmosphere in Roker Park was electric. The half-time whistle blew and the ground was buzzing. I can't remember a thing about the second half but anything would be an anti-climax after that first 45 minutes.

Stephen Morrissey

Bye Bye Bryan

Manchester United got a shock when they came to Roker Park in 1986. They were the Cup holders but Sunderland nearly knocked them out in a tough match at Roker. Bryan Robson had just come back from injury and he was sent off after he clashed with Barry Venison. The two players went in for a ball and while they both lay on the ground Robson hit out at Venison. The England captain left the field in disgrace. Sunderland should have won the match late on but Howard Gayle missed the goal completely when he was only a few yards out.

Ronnie McGuire

Highs and Lows

I don't think I have ever felt so low than after the Play-off game against Newcastle at Roker. One minute we were celebrating a penalty the next we were silent as Paul Hardyman's kick was saved and then he was sent off. That match was the most tense I can remember at Roker Park. There was so much at stake and it was made even worse by the fact we were playing the old enemy. That depression was replaced by elation when we won the second leg at St James'. I was listening on the radio and I was jumping around the house when Gates and Gabbiadini scored.

Karen Johnson

Sunderland's Nick Pickering and Paul McGrath of Manchester United in the mid 1980s. There have been many memorable clashes between the two great clubs over the years.

The Usual Suspects – Four staunch Sunderland supporters. Left to right: Neil Henderson, Ray Hassan, Tariq Ahmed and Andrew Clark.

Ringside Seats

My sister worked for Sunderland and got me and my friends some complimentary tickets for a match against Barnsley. We got our tickets from the main office but our seats were for the Clock Stand. It was just before the kick-off and we would have missed the start of the game if we had walked round the ground. So my sister led us through the Main Stand, on to the track and around the pitch to the Clock Stand. The teams were on the pitch at the time and I was praying for someone to knock it past Tony Norman so I could have a kickabout and knock it back to one of the players. I've never been so close to the players. It almost felt like we were warming-up with them. Once we got to our seats the day could have ended then and I would have gone home happy. The game itself was great. Mickey Gray was making his home debut and he scored in the first minute with his first kick.

Ray Hassan

The Final Match

I will always think of Sunderland's final game at Roker Park as the Everton match. I enjoyed the Liverpool game but there was nothing to play for. Against Everton it was all or nothing and Sunderland left the old stadium in style. Chris Waddle's free kick will go down as one of the great goals scored at Roker. I will never forget the way he ran towards the Fulwell End to celebrate. As a Sunderland supporter himself as a boy you could see the goal meant a lot to him as well.

Stephen Morrissey

The final whistle at Roker Park. The Sunderland and Everton players shake hands at the end of the last ever League game at the famous old stadium.

CHAPTER 4

Ha' Way The Lasses

he streets were crowded with people of every shape, size and age. Little babies were hoisted oulder-high by their over-zealous fathers and shaken almost like football rattles. The .thusiastic crowds lined the streets for miles, having waited for a long time, most of them essed in red and white and holding banners aloft … If supporters are the blood of a football .b, then Sunderland should never require a transfusion.

nny Watson, wife of 1973 Cup hero Dave.

lady footballer shows the nderland players how it's .e.

Argus' Girl

My father was Jack Anderson, the first Argus who wrote in the *Sunderland Echo*. From a very early age I became interested in football. My mother was a season ticket holder after the First World War and so were a number of her friends. My grandmother lived in Hampden Road near to Roker Park and I would be left with her while my mother went off to the match. I would howl at the window because I wanted to go to the match with her. I was told I couldn't go because I didn't have a ticket. This was in the 1920s. The first time I set off to go to Roker Park was when I was three-years-old. Someone hadn't shut the door properly and I got out of my grandmother's. Charlie Buchan and Arthur Andrews were coming up the street and they

recognised me as Jack Anderson's daughter. They came over to me and said, 'Where are you off to Marjorie?'

'I'm off to Roker Park for a ticket', I told them.

I first went to the match when I was eight. By half-time I was a bit fed up and started running up and down the stairs of the grandstand. When I got older I would go to all the games with my father. For away games we would travel with the team and I got to know all the players. They would often come to my father for advice. He would criticise them in the *Echo* but he felt he only did it when they needed it. The only player who didn't like criticism was Patsy Gallacher. He would bring his children to Roker Methodists' Sunday School where I taught and if my dad had criticised him in the *Football Echo* on the Saturday night he wouldn't talk to me on the Sunday. Sometimes my dad would write something that the

Jack Anderson, the *Sunderland Echo*'s first Argus with daughters Marjorie (right) and Muriel. In 1940 t war effort had first call on the services of the football correspondent and his family.

rectors didn't like and he wasn't
lowed to travel with the team for a
hile.

There were some transfers which took
ace in our front room. The manager at
at time, Johnny Cochrane would
ing players to our house to complete
ansfers away from Roker Park so no
ne would find out about the signing.
e once introduced my father as Mr
nith a butcher who knew nothing
out football. Johnny Cochrane liked
drink but in our house my mother
fused to give him alcohol. She gave
m a cup of tea instead but he had a
tle bottle of whisky which he poured
to the cup. She said he wouldn't even
t a cup of tea in future.

My father was a correspondent for
early all the nationals and I would
one over his reports to the
wspapers. Once there was another
urnalist at Roker Park and my father
d him I would phone over his copy as
ll. This reporter said, 'She won't be
le to read my writing.' My father
lied, 'Don't worry she knows more
out football than you do.' When
nderland won the League
ampionship in 1936 I was at the
lebration dinner at the Rink. The
lowing year I was at the celebrations
the Cup Final win. That night I
nk champagne out of the FA Cup. I
nt to every game in the Cup run of
37. I would always send a telegram to
ich Carter before each match to wish
n luck. On the day of the Final it
ln't arrive until just before the kick-
. There was panic stations when it
ked like it wasn't going to arrive.

rjorie Curtis

Bowler Basher

My mother was a big football fan.
When she was a teacher during
the First World War she taught the lads
football and organised the school team.
She would wash the strips herself
because some of the mothers wouldn't
do it. She would go to Roker Park with
my father who was also an avid fan. She
got so excited during one match, she
bashed in a man's bowler hat who was
standing in front of her. The thrill of
her life was when we won the Cup in
1973. When the team came back to
Sunderland we went to Vardy's Garage
on Durham Road. When the open top
coach came past she jumped into the
road and cheered them on.

Joan Pace

What's Going On

The first matches I went to were at
Whitley Bay but I would only see
the second half. It was free to get in at
half-time and that's when we would go.
Then I went to St James' Park to see
Newcastle. They got beat 2-1 although I
couldn't see a thing because I was
standing on the terraces. The only time
I saw the ball was when it was up in the
air. I was standing behind the goal and
when the teams swapped ends in the
second half I thought we would all
move behind the other goal. When I
met Dave, who became my husband, I
got converted to Sunderland.

Lesley Harrison

Cover girls – Young supporters in the late 1970s sport the badges of their favourite players.

Learning the Trade

The first game I went to was against Liverpool in 1985. A few months before Sunderland had played them at Roker and the game had to be abandoned at half-time. My first match was the re-arranged game and it was cheaper to get in. I stood in the Main Stand paddock and could hardly see a thing. I felt my eyes were about level with the knees of the players. All I could see were throw-ins and the substitutes warming up. It was at the time when there were fences in the paddocks and that didn't help either. The next match I went to was the last game in the Third Division when Sunderland won the Championship. I enjoyed the night but I wasn't used to standing for so long. I was wearing a pair of boots that were absolutely killing me by the end of the game. It took me few matches before I fully understood the rules. During a Cup game Sunderland were leading by a few goals and it looked like we were going to score more. When I said, 'This will do our goal difference some good', all my friends started laughing at me.

Tracy Ahmed

Seeing a Legend

The only time I went to Roker Park was to see Stanley Matthews. He was playing for Blackpool in the 1950s was packed and I couldn't see the pitch never mind Matthews. Ronnie, my husband, paid a young lad a few pence so I could stand in his space, but I still couldn't see. Then Ronnie lifted me up and I saw Matthews. I then said to my husband, 'I've seen him so let's go home.'

Elizabeth Clark

Before Boyfriends

I went to a lot of games when I was a teenager in the early 1960s. Once you started getting yourself a boyfriend you stopped going, especially if he hadn't the same interest as you did. We would always stand at the back and never go down the front. At the front it was too packed. Sometimes the ground was so full you couldn't breathe. There was just no space.

Audrey Henderson

Daytime

We lived in Park Avenue near St Andrew's church and Sunderland owned houses in the street where the players would stay. My son John, when he was young, would play with some of the Sunderland players. He would play football with Stan Anderson because he only had a little girl and said he didn't know any girls' games. John would also play in the garden with Len Shackleton.

Marjorie Curtis

Hot Seats

At Turf Moor in the 1972-73 season we were in the stand behind the goal and they had the heaters on and it was roasting. It was April and a warm night and they had this ducted warm air blowing through the stands. I've been at plenty of grounds where I wanted to be warmer but this was too much.

Lesley Harrison

Changing Times

From the early '60s I travelled all over the country to watch Sunderland. We used to go on a coach run from The Blandford pub in the town centre. There was never any trouble in those days. Then all of a sudden – over night – things changed. For a long time you could not mix with opposing supporters for fear of trouble.

Margaret Calvert

The One and Only

I listen for Sunderland's results after every game but I only went to one match at Roker Park. I wanted to see what it was like. It was a night match and I think the way the pitch was lit up by the floodlights made it more special. I made sure I was well wrapped-up and wore my sheepskin coat. I had a flask of coffee for half-time.

Pauline Clark

Get Me to the Church

We waited until the fixture list came out in June before we booked our wedding day. We looked at the fixtures and chose 12 October 1974 when Sunderland were away to Bristol City. We didn't fancy going to that game, although we still listened for the result. The bridesmaids wore red and white dresses and the only thing that was missing were numbers on the back. We only had a few days honeymoon in the Lake District before we were back to Sunderland on the Tuesday night to see them play Sheffield Wednesday.

Lesley Harrison

Welcome Visits

Over the years I've made friends with loads of away supporters. They call at my pub (The Cambridge) whenever they are in the region even when their teams have not been at Roker. In the 1996-97 season seven Chelsea lads I know came in after they had been to St James' and some old friends from West Ham called after playing at Middlesbrough.

Margaret Calvert

Margaret Calvert and partner Norman Pounder behind the bar of The Cambridge. This Fulwell Road pu is a popular watering hole for Sunderland supporters on matchdays.

The wedding day of Lesley and Dave Harrison in 1974. The bridesmaids are in Sunderland's colours of red & white. Left to right: Ray Hutchinson, Teresa Hutchinson, Chris Nelson, Julie Merriman, Dave, Lesley, Elaine James, Steve Jackson.

Pregnant Pause

When Sunderland played Derby County at the beginning of the 1992-93 season I was a few months pregnant and often felt faint. I was standing in the Roker End and after a few minutes I needed to sit down. Sunderland were getting beat at the time and while I was sitting on the terraces feeling very unwell a supporter behind me said, 'Cheer up it's not that bad – we'll get a goal soon.'

Tracy Ahmed

Happy Days

Winning promotion to the Premiership at the end of the 1995-96 season were great times. Before the last match at home we were already assured of going up but a point against West Brom would see us crowned Champions. Before the match, flags were being sold and there was a really happy atmosphere. The game itself was uneventful and it ended 0-0 but we were Champions and a rendition of *Cheer Up Peter Reid* must have been heard for miles. After the match the

Sunderland fanatic Andrea Lane.

players and Peter Reid ran on to the pitch in twos. When Bally lifted the trophy up it was such a good feeling. Then all the singing began and the players did a lap of honour, this was such a proud moment and one I know I will never forget.

Andrea Lane

What a Start

The first game I went to was at Tottenham in 1990. It was a cold rainy day, and a friend had his umbrella confiscated at the entrance to the ground. We were standing behind the goal and there was plenty of action. There were six goals with the score finishing 3-3. What a game to start with. During the celebrations for a Sunderland goal I almost lost an earring in the jostle of the excitement. Gary Lineker scored the last goal in the dying seconds of injury-time. Immediately after the game I was told that it was not normal to see six goals at a match. This one had been something special and one of my friends said it was one of the best games he had ever seen. I was told that I would never be able to go to a match again because my expectations would be too high. To this day, I am still told that I was spoiled in my introduction to football.

Karen Henderson

CHAPTER 5

The Lads on Tour

*or me the real stars of the day were red and white – and despite how well they fought, how
agnificently they gave everything, I don't mean the Sunderland players. The hordes who
llow them, lift them, and love them, are the reason I remember this game.*

rank McGhee, *Daily Mirror*, after Sunderland's triumph over Leeds in 1973.

ob Robinson (centre with the rattle) and workmates from JL Thompson's Manor Quay Yard in London
r the Cup game against Spurs in 1950.

Little House on Tour

The Divan in Hendon Road was the starting point for countless trips to away matches run by Tommy Little.

Tommy Little the landlord of The Divan public house in Hendon Road used to run trips to away matches. Tommy was a little, stocky guy and a real character. Before and after the Second World War he organised transport to Sunderland games all round the country. Some journeys such as to The Dell at Southampton had to set off late on a Friday night. In the pre-motorway days they had to travel through the night to get there in time for the Saturday afternoon kick-off.

Billy Barker

Excursion to Leeds and Huddersfield.
HUDDERSFIELD v SUNDERLAND
Saturday, December 14th, 1935

Latest Tourist Stock with Buffett cars, every seat guaranteed, accommodation specially reserved for parties. Passengers may return from Huddersfield to Leeds after the match by 5-47 train, without extra cost.

LEEDS 8/-   HUDDERSFIELD 9/-

Sunderland dep. 8-55 a.m. arr. Leeds 11-50 a.m   arr. Huddersfield 12-30 p.m.
Huddersfield dep. 11-15 p.m. Leeds (New) dep. 11-59 p.m, Arr Sunderland 2-43 a.m,

APPLY—TOMMY LITTLE, 11 HENDON VALLEY ROAD, SUNDERLAND.

An advert in the Sunderland programme in December 1935 for a trip to Huddersfield run by Tommy Little. In this instance the party travelled by train.

To Spurs for Thirty Bob

The first away match I went to was down at Tottenham in 1950. For thirty bob we got a coach from Easington Lane, a ticket for the game and a meal at Lyons Corner Cafe. At the cafe there was a quartet playing and when they saw us they started playing *The Blaydon Races*. At the game Sunderland scored in the first few minutes. I turned to a Spurs' supporter next to me and said we would score six today and he agreed. In those days there was no segregation and you could stand next to the opposing fans with no trouble. As it turned out we didn't score again, Tottenham won 5-1 and we left the ground with our tails between our legs. Sunderland's goal was scored by the centre forward Dickie Davis but then he got an old fashioned shoulder charge from their centre half and was injured for the rest of the game. There were no substitutes then.

Jack Sanderson

The Big Cheese Affair

When we were down at Tottenham for the Cup tie in 1950 a man came into the pub we were in with an offer we could not refuse. He asked if anyone wanted to buy some cheese. As cheese was still rationed at this time there were plenty of takers. We went outside and bought big 9lb pieces of cheese from the back of his lorry. When we got back to Sunderland we read in the newspapers that a lorry with $2\frac{1}{2}$ tons

A party of shipwrights and joiners from JL Thompson's shipyard in Trafalgar Square before the Cup tie at Spurs in 1950.

of red cheese had gone missing the day before the Spurs game while en route from Newcastle to Sunderland. My mam went mad with my dad for bringing the cheese into the house. She cut the cheese up into small pieces and disposed of it by all sorts of means – including flushing it down the toilet.

Bob Robinson

George Forster showing where his allegiance lies. George is a leading light of Sunderland Supporters' Association.

Friendly Opposition

For years I hardly missed an away match. I was at Davey Browns and should have worked overtime on a Saturday but I had a good foreman who let me off if I worked a Sunday. When we went to an away game we would stay in the town till about 11 o'clock at night. We had some great times away from home. A famous haunt of ours was the Cheshire Cheese in Manchester. I would get up on stage and go through my repertoire of songs. When we went to West Brom we would go to the Throstles Club. Their fans always made us very welcome. We rarely saw

Sunderland win away from home but we would enjoy ourselves.

George Forster

Tour of Britain

For years we wouldn't book our holidays without first looking at the fixture list. In the 1973-74 season we went away in a camper van for a fortnight to combine a holiday with watching Sunderland play. We watched the match at home on the Saturday then set off. We first went to Nottingham and saw Sunderland play Notts County. Then we went to Scotland coming back for another game at Roker against Cardiff City. Next it was off to Cornwall followed by a match at Portsmouth and then back home.

Lesley Harrison

The Long Journey Home

In the late 1960s I went to several away matches with my friends. It was a great experience visiting other towns because going away on holidays was a rarity in those days. We were all teenagers and several of us were under age drinkers, but we looked forward to the night out after the game. After one game against Liverpool we stopped off at a pub in Manchester. We had a great night and most of us were worse for wear with drink. Near the end of the night a photographer came into the pub and he was taking 'instant pictures' – a bit of a novelty in those days. Many supporters left the pub to make their way to their coaches but several of us stayed behind to be photographed. We were a few minutes late for the agreed leaving time and our coach had gone. The alcohol softened the blow of being stranded in the middle of Manchester at about 11.30 p.m. on a Saturday night with very little money. But the reality of the problem dawned on seven teenagers during a hard night of sobering up.

Several incidents during the long journey home stand out in my memory. We boarded a train to Preston without tickets and the seven of us crammed into a small toilet to avoid the guard. It seemed a long journey and it was in the wrong direction! We arrived at Preston and walked in circles for about two hours before asking a policeman at a small station if he could help but he couldn't. We found a bus shelter where we slept for a while before we made our way to a motorway where we walked for several hours to Lancaster. Here we again approached the police, this time at a large station. They said they could help but the money for the fares home would have to be collected from only one home in Sunderland to save the inconvenience of visiting seven houses. None of us could agree to that because we knew that none of our families would have that sort of money.

We made our way home by train. We paid some of the way but avoided paying on some trains. At a small station at Lancaster the porter heard of our predicament and opened the waiting room for us. It was late on Sunday afternoon and we were tired and hungry. It seemed to me that most of us were asleep when the porter returned with a can full of tea and sandwiches cut into quarters which was his bait. He placed them on the table and said he'd brought something for us to eat. At first none of us stirred until he left and shut the door. Everybody suddenly 'woke up' at the same time and there was a stampede for the bait led by Geordie Smith who had been snoring only a few seconds previously. We finally arrived home on Bank Holiday Monday morning. When we got off the train at Seaburn Station, one of the lads, Ian Farrer, kissed the ground with relief.

Peter Gibson

One of the photographs taken in Manchester which caused seven supporters to miss their coach home. Left to right: Peter Gibson, Tommy 'Bomber' Keegan, Tucker Mooney. Tucker did manage to catch the bus but could not persuade the driver to wait for his friends.

Boarding the Old Trafford-bound coach outside the Downhill Workmen's Club, Sunderland, in the 1990-91 season.

Old Trafford Sideshows

Sunderland's visit to Old Trafford in January 1991 provided few happy memories. United stormed into a 3-0 lead by half-time. Young full back Paul Williams was handed his full debut against the side that were soon to dominate English football. Lee Sharpe was in devastating form and the score could have been even worse.

Sunderland rallied in the second half and there were no further goals. As the Sunderland supporters were making their way from the ground to cars and coaches they tried to lift their spirits. There was a man painting his house and a crazy chant went up, 'Paint when you're winning, you only paint when you're winning.' Another local was driving slowing through the travelling

fans on a moped when a Sunderland man jumped on the pillion. The surprised driver almost did a wheelie with his unexpected passenger.

Jackie Turnbull

Whose Afraid of Giggs & Co

One of my first away games was Manchester United in the third round of the FA Cup. When we arrived in Manchester, the first thing I noticed when I got off the coach was Old Trafford. It was huge, about twice the size of Roker Park and it was so neat and tidy. I just stood staring at it for a few minutes. The next thing I remember noticing was seeing nearly every Sunderland fan in Manchester standing on the streets because they

ouldn't get in the pubs. As I was
etting ready to walk to the ground an
ld man came up to me and when he
aw my Sunderland top he said are you
ure you want to watch this, it will be
-0 to United. He looked at me as if to
ay I was mental for supporting
underland. What an idiot he was.
Nicky Butt gave United the lead but
oals from Craig Russell and Steve
Agnew put us ahead. The next thing I
emember is just jumping on people and
creaming. A strange man kissed my
ad. Football does weird things to
eople. This game was proving to be
near heaven until Cantona ended up
qualising. I have never heard 8,000
eople make so much noise. Even Alex
erguson said how lucky United were
nd how great the Sunderland fans
ere. That day to me is what football is
bout.

Andrea Lane

Charlie Crushes Canaries

When Sunderland were drawn
against Norwich away in the FA
Cup in 1961 we took a huge following
to Carrow Road. On the morning of the
game I saw Harry Hooper and I told him
when we got a corner to put the ball on
Charlie Hurley's head. During the game
I think we only got one corner and as
usual Charlie made his way up for it.
When he started to make his run he had
three Norwich players clinging on to
him, yet he still got to the ball first and
headed home a beauty. What a goal –
what a player. I ended up watching from
the cinder track in the second half and
when the final whistle blew I was on the
pitch. I tried to catch up with Charlie
but I was left trailing behind. When I
went back to work at Greenwell's on the
Monday morning a cheer went up. One

A view from the Sunderland supporters' enclosure at Old Trafford on 12 January 1991. The old Stretford
End is in the background in the days before it was all-seated.

Dennis Martin (with top hat) tries catching up Charlie Hurley at the end of the 1961 Cup tie at Norwich

Dennis Martin (right) working on his stall at Sunderland fish quay in the summer of 1997.

f the lads had a copy of the *Daily Mail* nd there was a photograph of me on ne pitch. They had my life all week.

Dennis Martin

Monty Blinder

My first away match was at Huddersfield in December 1962. I ent with my uncle on a coach rganised by Boldon Club. Huddersfield riped the floor with us in the first half ut they couldn't score. I think Montgomery had the goal boarded up. He had a blinder and some people say it was his best ever game for Sunderland. t was 0-0 at half-time then five minutes nto the second half we were winning -0 and the game was as good as over. Cloughie latched on to a couple of hrough balls and scored twice. George Mulhall got a third later in the game. On the way back the coach stopped at a

pub in Leeds at about 7 o'clock and all the men went in. I was only thirteen so I stayed in the bus until about 11 o'clock when they came back and we set off for home.

Dave Harrison

Hat Trick

In the early 1960s it was rare to see anything other than a scarf, rattle or rosette in club colours. But for a game at Huddersfield in December 1962 I wore a paper mache top hat bought for 9/- at a theatrical goods shop opposite The Empire. It was painted in red and white stripes and was still wet from the night before. My spectacles had the lenses covered with red and white stripes with slots to see through. Impressed by my attire a press guy handed me a complimentary ticket for the seats. I offered it to the lads I was with but we

A group of supporters from Southwick Social Club on their way to Norwich for the FA Cup tie in 1961.

Norman Howey's famous sons: former Sunderland now Burnley man Lee and Steven of Newcastle and England.

Invasion of Leeds

I was at Elland Road for Leeds United's largest ever attendance. It was in the FA Cup in 1967. The teams had drawn 1-1 at Roker and the replay at Leeds drew a record crowd. I was in the paddock of the main stand at Elland Road and looking across the ground you could see dozens of fans climbing over a wall to get in. That game also ended in a draw and there was a second replay at Boothferry Park, Hull. Leeds were leading 1-0 then about twelve minutes from the end Alan Gauden equalised. Sunderland came forward much more and looked like they could go on to win the match. Then Leeds played a long ball up field in the final minute and one of their players went down in the penalty box. The referee was miles away from the incident but he couldn't get to the penalty spot fast enough. Leeds scored and went into the lead. George Herd got sent off for dissent and then George Mulhall also went for telling the linesman where to stick his flag. So Sunderland finished the game with nine all preferred to stand so I kept the ticket. It was a memorable game with Sunderland winning 3-0. Norman Howey (whose sons played for Sunderland and Newcastle) and I ran on the pitch at the end of the game to walk back to the tunnel with Cloughie. I put the top hat on his head. Doug Weatherall writing in the *Daily Herald* wrote the cap that the England International Selectors refused to give Brian Clough was placed on his head in the form of a top hat by two enthusiastic supporters. 'Onlooker' in the *Echo* commented on a fan attending the game with 'red and white eyes.'

Mickey Bute

Nº 710

Huddersfield Town A.F.C., Ltd.

Complimentary Ticket

Turnstile 27
To be given up on
Entrance to Stand B

Match v............................

Date......................19...

Kick-off............p.m.

A. Galvin, Secretary
E. Boot, Manager

The seat t
for the gan
Huddersfi
1962. It w
unused be
the recipie
preferred t
stand with
mates on t
terraces.

A Sunderland supporter in the Forest End. Colin Maughan (left) punches the air with a Nottingham Forest fan at the City Ground for Sunderland's visit on the final day of the 1993-94 season.

men. I was very bitter after that result and very angry towards the referee.

Dave Harrison

The Men in Black

The FA Cup tie against Burnley in 1979 was postponed a number of times because of bad weather. When it finally got the go ahead we took a half day from the shipyards and travelled down by car. We stopped at a pub just outside of Burnley before the game. We walked in the bar and saw five or six men all dressed in black with cowboy hats. There was no way we could get out and just hoped these mad looking characters did not start trouble. 'Alright lads, down for the match?' one of them said in an unmistakable East Durham

accent. The men in black were Sunderland supporters.

Michael Stephenson

The Lads Take Liverpool

One of the best away days I ever went on was the Liverpool game in 1981. Sunderland needed to win at Anfield in the last game of the season to ensure First Division survival. The terraces behind the goal opposite the Kop End were packed with Sunderland supporters. In the middle of these, standing on a fence, or on somebody's shoulders, was a fat skinhead dressed as the Pope. He had a remarkable resemblance to John Paul II. Dressed in his silk robes and skull cap, he acted the part by blessing the crowd. The

For many years the bus company Cowell Brothers of Southwick provided transport for Sunderland fan travelling away from home. Here are two drivers, with their buses, on Cup Final day in 1937.

Sunderland and England full back, Steve Whitworth was spotted in the stand adjoining ours. Up went the chant of, 'One Stevie Whitworth, there's only one ...' He gave us a wave in acknowledgement with a look of astonishment at the size of the Wearside following. Just before the kick-off the Liverpool boss, Bob Paisley was presented with yet another Manager of the Month award and the Sunderland supporters joined in the rousing reception he was given. The chant went up, 'Geordie, Geordie ...' recalling his Hetton roots. There was one song which echoed all around Anfield before and during the match.

In Dublin's fair city where the girls are so pretty
I first set my eyes on sweet Molly Malone
She wheeled her wheelbarrow
Through streets broad and narrow
Crying ... Sunderland ... Sunderland

The famous Kop was strangely quite all afternoon and when Stan Cummins scored a brilliant goal to give Sunderland the lead it silenced the home supporters for good. Sunderland hung on to their lead to the final whistle to record a great win.

Mark Taylor

Fearing for our Lives

The only match I ever left before the end was at Stamford Bridge in the semi-final of the Milk Cup in 1985. That was because we feared for our lives. We had bought our tickets at Roker Park and expected to be with the Sunderland fans. However, we were in the West Stand with the home supporters. We were surrounded by Chelsea fans and it was very frightening.

There were a couple of their fans around us who were reasonable but the rest created a very intimidating atmosphere. Sunderland went a goal behind then Clive Walker equalised and then put us in front. By now some of the Chelsea fanatics had run on to the pitch and the police had to take them away. Colin West scored Sunderland's third goal and but jumped a police horse to head it in. We decided to leave just after Pat Nevin pulled a goal back five minutes before full time. A couple of Chelsea fans were gracious in defeat but they warned us to be careful when we left the ground. They told us it would be better not to go to Fulham Broadway tube station because that's where the thugs would be waiting. We were advised to walk past them, keep our mouth shut and go on to Sloan Square station. We got to Sloan Square tube station and a train pulled in packed with men wearing blue and white. One of the Sunderland fans who was with us said, 'Do you think they are Chelsea supporters?' My husband replied, 'Just shout come on you reds and you will soon find out.'

Lesley Harrison

Enough's Enough

The thing which disappointed me most that night was that we couldn't celebrate our win. We had got to Wembley fair and square but we had to sneak away as if we had pinched something. I've never been back to Chelsea.

Dave Harrison

Friendlier Times at the Bridge

At Chelsea they had the normal stalls where you bought beer and burgers, then they had these little tuck shops where you could buy 10p 'mix-ups' and bags of sweets. They had lovely wine gums.

Ray Hassan

In a Sea of Blue

I watched the Sunderland versus Chelsea Cup replay in 1992 on a telly in a pub in Hertford, just north of London. I work in London and couldn't get time off to go back home for the match. So Sky TV coverage had to do. I got to the pub just before kick-off. I was wearing my treasured home shirt and as I walked into the pub I was greeted by the sight of nine or ten Chelsea shirts. Everyone went quiet and looked at me. I walked to the bar and ordered a drink. I sat at the only available seat, at a table with two Chelsea fans. The first thing one of them said was, 'We should stuff your lot, tonight.' Then he smiled and said, 'But knowing how bad we are, we probably won't.' They turned out to be all right. We ended up buying rounds and had a good night. The funny thing about meeting other football fans is that they're all the same. It doesn't matter who you support, everyone thinks that their team is rubbish, but loves them anyway. It was 1-0 to Sunderland for most of the match after a Davenport screamer. Then with a few minutes to go, Dennis Wise equalised. I was gutted. The Chelsea lads started up a chorus of 'Your round! Your round!' I got up and reluctantly went to the bar. As I ordered the drinks I saw Sunderland take a corner and the next thing I knew the ball was in the net. It was just as well I didn't have a drink in my hand because it would have gone all over. The pub was silent again. I think I might have got a bit cocky at that point and asked if anyone wanted crisps or peanuts with their drinks. I can't repeat the replies.

Neil Henderson

Over the Wall

In 1955 Sunderland played Newcastle twice in two days. In the first game at Roker Park on Boxing Day Sunderland were beaten 6-1. After that defeat Sunderland went out and bought the Burnley centre forward Bill Holden. After the defeat at Roker I wasn't going to go to Newcastle but after Holden was signed a friend and I decided to go. We were late getting to St James' Park and the gates were shut and the police were moving people away from the ground. A little fella came up to us and said he would get us into the ground. We started walking up to Leazes Park and this sergeant on a police horse came towards us and said we should move off. The little guy said, 'What are you playing at. Get your horse off my foot.' The policeman pointed in the direction he wanted us to go but the guy stood his ground and said, 'I'm a citizen of Newcastle and nothing prevents me going up to Leazes Park.' So we waited

until the policeman had gone and the little guy asked a kid to help him get into the ground. He lifted the kid on to a tree so he could jump over the wall of the stadium and then open a gate. The boy got in, opened a gate and about thirty of us got into the ground like this.

George Hoare

Up on the Roof

I supported Sunderland and Newcastle and would go to Roker or St James' Park depending on what was the best game. I always went to the derby matches but there was one game in the 1960s at St James' I couldn't get in because the ground was full. So I climbed on the roof of one of the houses overlooking the ground and watched the game from there. I had a suit on because I was going out afterwards but when I climbed down I was absolutely filthy and covered in soot from the chimneys.

Ron Collins

Tyneside Rumours

I went to Newcastle in 1964 to see Sunderland play. The weather was terrible and it had been pouring down all day. We were standing in the queue outside St James' Park when someone walked past and said the game was off because the pitch was waterlogged. Everyone around us just walked away and we went back to the station to

...ord Beresford kicks-off a friendly between Sunderland and Newcastle on 27 September 1904. The ...ouses that overlooked the ground gave their occupants a prime view of the action. This was the case ...ght up to recent times.

...atch the train back to Sunderland. When I got home I found out that the ...ame had been played and that it was ...ust a rumour that the game was off. My ...ad couldn't stop laughing when he ...ound out what I had done.

...Harry Clark

Alternative Entertainment

It was a foggy morning when two car loads set off to Newcastle for the ...derby game two days after Christmas in ...965. Calling in a pub at opening time ...ve watched the news on TV to find, as ...ve had anticipated, the game was ...cancelled due to the bad weather. We ...agreed to go back to Sunderland for a ...drink. 'What's on at Farra?' (Farringdon

Club) someone asked. 'Bobby Knoxall was on yesterday. Tonight a German gadgy's on, Englebert Humptydonk or somebody.' We decided to go to the Farringdon Club. It was a surprise to arrive at Farra to find the 'German' was Jerry Dorsey who we all were sick of seeing around the clubs. 'Well you were half right with the Gerry', somebody said. Englebert Humperdink topped the charts with his first hit *Please Release Me* about four months later.

Mickey Bute

Red & White Eyes

For the derby game at St James' Park in 1966 I wore a red and white shirt, red and white jockey's hat, scarf, rosette,

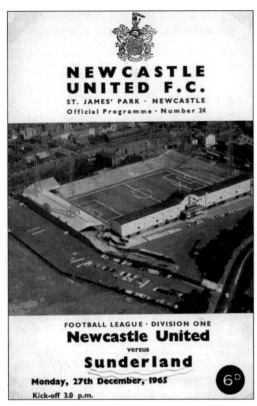

The programme for Sunderland's visit to St James' Park in December 1965. The match was called off on the morning of the game and was re-arranged a week later.

The First and the Last

I went to my first derby at St James' Park in January 1971 for a 'friendly'. I was fifteen at the time and went along with two friends from school. I can't remember much about the game but I recall coming out of the Gallowgate End early to avoid trouble. It was too late as hundreds of Newcastle skinheads had already come out of the Leazes End and had gathered outside our end. The three of us made our way down the zigzag steps of the old terracing. When we reached the bottom my mates decided it would be safer to return to the bulk of the Sunderland support (a few thousand strong). I decided it was safer to leave now, plus I had my leg in plaster and did not fancy going back up all the steps. I began to make my way through the army of shaven-headed Newcastle supporters. They all seemed to be blokes in their thirties and forties. Of course I did not have any colours on and just hoped I could slip down to the railway station without being rumbled. I dreaded anyone asking me the time! That was the traditional way rival supporters, with their 'foreign' accents, are uncovered. There was a thought in my mind if they did find out where my allegiance lay these big men would not hit a little, skinny kid. But I didn't know. I was just passing The Strawberry pub when I was sent flat on my back. I didn't see a flat-capped policeman walking through the crowd against the flow and I bounced off him. He just carried on and I managed to get up with my plastered leg undamaged and continued on to the station. I must have

and sun glasses painted red and white with little holes in them so I could see. I looked like a red and white stick of candy rock. I walked up Pilgrim Street dressed like that and all I got was banter and chat. Go into Newcastle today and say you are a Sunderland supporter and you are asking for trouble.

Dave Harrison

vent on a long detour because by the time I reached the Central Station it vas late and police dogs had cleared the rea. I got a train home with no further nishaps. I found out on the following Monday at school that one of my friends had walked round a corner straight into a giant fist. I've only been back to St ames' once since – to see a Bob Dylan oncert.

ackie Turnbull

Sunderland supporters on tour.

Party Day

For the final match of the 1995-96 season we travelled to Tranmere and despite getting beat 2-0 there was a carnival atmosphere. At the end of the match almost every Sunderland fan ran on the pitch and started singing. What a sight – a sea of red and white. What a season.

Andrea Lane

No Sight, No Taste & No Points

On New Years' Eve 1989 I was talked into going to the following day's match at Hull City. As we were leaving early in the morning I was put up on the settee of one of my mates. I put my contact lenses in two glasses of water. I was not expecting to stay out so I did not have the case to keep them in. Next morning I awoke to find an early bird had cleaned up the house and unwittingly poured my lenses down the sink. So it was with a hangover and very

little vision that I watched the action at Boothferry Park. I did manage to see Gordon Armstrong's penalty miss as Sunderland went down 2-3 to a poor Hull side. One other lasting memory of the Hull trip was the pies at the ground. The contents didn't look like normal meat: the texture was like cardboard, it was grey looking and the shape of the chunks were too regular to be 'natural' meat. I'm sure clubs keep special pies for away supporters.

Tommy Allen

Hold the Bus

Billy Bremner's testimonial was against Sunderland at Elland Road in May 1974. Sunderland lined up with almost the Cup winning side. We missed the coach as it left Park Lane

Sunderland supporters enjoying the sunshine at Tranmere at the last game of the season in 1996.

The Red & White Army takes over Prenton Park on the last day of the promotion season.

The Black Cat hits Thornton Heath High Street on their way to Selhurst Park.

nd had to 'intercept' it opposite underland Infirmary. Four of us got out f my car to join the bus. Big Harry, the rganiser of the trip, was furious about s being so late. Worse was to follow, owever, as we eventually settled down nd got the cards out. Bobby the Bish Kirtlan) couldn't find his coat with his noney (£60) in. We were at Scotch Corner by the time someone convinced im that he got on without his coat. Big Harry thought it was a wind-up when e was asked to go back but eventually e relented. On returning to underland the Bish's coat was still on op of my car where he had left it and he 60 quid was still in the top pocket.

Mickey Bute

Those Were the Days

I enjoyed going to away matches because I enjoyed mixing with other fans. You would have a drink and chat with away supporters. Even when they introduced limited segregation I would still buy a ticket for the home end. I miss not mixing with other fans. When you go to an away ground today you are normally stuck in the worst part of the stadium where it is difficult to see. You are marched in like a criminal and marched out like a criminal. I could never understand that just because I wanted to go to a football match that I should be treated like this. I haven't done anything wrong but I can't go into

93

Dave Harrison – Red & White through and through. He has travelled the length and breadth of the country following The Lads.

a pub, I've got to be searched, do what I am told, go here, go there, etc, etc.

Dave Harrison

Unlucky

After the 1973 Cup run travelling to away matches became even more popular. A group of us from the Park Inn formed the Sunderland Travellers' Club. Harry Emery, the chairman, had a standing bet with Brian Trewitt (owner of bookmakers Gus Carters) on Vic Halom scoring a hat-trick with odds of 50/1. The bet was placed every Saturday Vic played. In one game against Millwall in February 1974 Halom scored

twice in the first half and Harry said, 'I'm on a winner here.' However, the hat-trick failed to materialise. As it happened the only hat-trick Halom scored for Sunderland was in a 3-0 win against Derby County in the League Cup. As that game was played mid-week Harry still lost out as his bet was only placed on Saturdays. Eddie Goodwin, a regular on Sunderland Travellers' trips, was often the worse for wear after a visit to the Yates' Wine Lodges in various cities. Once, in Birmingham, Eddie, seeing a bus with red and white scarf clad occupants near to the Hawthorns, enquired, 'Is this bus going to the town? Somebody shouted yes and so Eddie got on. When Eddie said the town he meant Birmingham City centre for a night out. The journey seemed to take a long time and Eddie fell asleep. He was surprised when he was woken up and told to get off to find he was in Park Lane. Of course to any Sunderland supporter there is only one 'town'.

Mickey Bute

Pillow Talk

On 10 May 1997 we travelled by coach to Selhurst Park for the last game of the season against Wimbledon. We made fun of a teenage girl when she brought a fancy pillow out of her rucksack. It reminded me of the Charlie Brown character who carries his 'comfort' blanket everywhere he goes. She had the last laugh when she put the pillow to good use on the long journey home.

Tommy Allen

CHAPTER 6

Wembley Dreams

y arms ached, holding aloft the Cup. Every member of the team must have been moved,
it to me personally it meant so much more. This was my home town; these were my folk. I
is the local boy who had led the team to victory and brought home the Cup for which they
d been waiting for fifty years.

aich Carter, the first Sunderland captain to lift the FA Cup.

icky Gibson gets into the spirit of the occasion on FA Cup Final Day, 1992.

All Aboard

When the train carrying the team for the 1937 Cup Final left Sunderland there were crowds all along the railway line. People were throwing red and white streamers in front of the train. We were in the 7/6 seats for the Final which were in front of the Royal Box. They weren't under cover. The roof at that time didn't go right around the stadium or down to the pitch. Alex Hastings didn't play in the Final because of injury and he was sitting near us. At half-time, when Sunderland were 1-0 down, he was panicking about Sunderland getting beat. But I knew we would win.

Marjorie Curtis

Day Out in London

In 1937 I went to the Cup Final. There was so many trains. Many Sunderland firms had booked railway coaches for their workmen. I went with Redhead and Browns and train after train left Sunderland Station. When I turned up at the north end of the station the queue stretched right back to Mackies Corner. I had a bell stuck on to a stump of wood and I rang that bell all the way down to the platform. When we got to London we went into Lyons Cafe for our breakfast and we just mingled with the Preston supporters. We went up to the zoo until it was time for the match. At Wembley I was in the end where the goals were scored. After the match, when we got to King's Cross Station for the train back to Sunderland, I was amazed to see *Football Echos* being sold there. I bought one and put it in front of me on the table but remembered no more until the train pulled into Sunderland – I slept the journey back. Remember we had been awake all night and been around London more or less for the rest of the time apart from the match – I went out like a light.

Wilf Lathan

Raich Carter puts Sunderland into the lead at Wembley in 1937. At that time the roof did not offer shelter from the elements for all spectators.

The north end of Sunderland Central Railway Station. Queues stretched down to Fawcett Street when supporters started their journey to the Cup Final in 1937.

Footy Echo in London

The *Football Echo* was printed in Portsmouth straight after the Cup Final. It was flown up to London and sold in the streets to people who had been at the game only a few hours before.

Marjorie Curtis

The famous *Football Echo* ball shows its delight at the club's first FA Cup triumph.

Bigger & Bigger

At the start of the 1972-73 season there were big gaps on the terraces. As the Cup run progressed the crowds grew bigger and bigger until they were over fifty thousand with not a square inch of space.

John Yearnshire

The Start of the Dream

I went to the replay against Notts County in the first round of the Cup run in 1973 and Sunderland were pathetic. If some one had given you a million to one for Sunderland to win the Cup you wouldn't have backed them.

George Hoare

The Return of the King

Charlie Hurley came back to Roker Park for the fourth round of the Cup in 1973. He was manager of Reading and got a great reception from the crowd. Reading got a draw at Roker but we beat them in the replay.

Peter Gibson

Cup Favourites Beaten

The best game I ever went to was the Manchester City replay at Roker in the Cup in 1973. I had been at the first game at Maine Road where we drew to force a replay at home. We got back late from Manchester on the Saturday night but we were up at the crack of dawn to queue for tickets for the replay. It was a tremendous game and was end to end stuff. Sunderland won with goals from Billy Hughes (2) and Vic Halom. After we had beaten City I knew we were going to win the Cup.

Dave Harrison

Halom Rocket

The first goal against Manchester City took me by surprise. When Vic

Three-year-old Ian Affleck gets into the Cu Final spirit in 1973.

alom scored it took me a few seconds to realise it was a goal. The ball seemed to go into the angle between the upright and the cross bar and fit neatly into the corner. Then the ball was bouncing in the net and we then knew it was a goal. I couldn't believe we were 1-0 up against such a great side as Man City. That to me was the best game I ever saw at Roker Park.

Peter Gibson

For Whom The Bell Tolls

My dad and me were in the seats for the Cup game against Manchester City at Roker in 1973. We had a City supporter next to us who created a din with a bell. He was only silenced when Sunderland scored. When we got home we were all set to enjoy the highlights again on television. The only disappointment was that the pictures were in black and white because the floodlighting was not up to allowing colour transmission.

Geoff Pearson

Pennies From Heaven

When Sunderland drew at Manchester City in the Cup in 1973 I was desperate to go to the replay. The problem was I had no money. I was thirteen at the time and went to Southmoor School. On the day of the match I went round school and cadged pennies off my mates. I eventually collected enough to go. The gateman was surprised when I paid with a handful of copper.

Barry Rodgerson

Celebrations

I was on duty as a policeman for the replay against Man City at Roker in 1973. I was on guard in the counting house when Sunderland scored their third goal. We rushed outside to enjoy the wild celebrations.

John Yearnshire

Eerie Atmosphere

The atmosphere at the quarter-final against Luton in 1973 was strangely subdued. The crowd was big enough because me and a friend's young brother were pushed to the side of the Roker End. The young lad was Bruce Halliday who was later to play for Newcastle.

Geoff Pearson

Great Day at Hillsborough

I heard the draw for the semi-final in a lay-by near the Tyne Tunnel at 12 o'clock on the Monday afternoon. I wanted to be drawn against Wolves but we got Arsenal. I went to the semi at Hillsborough and was in tears that day. At the end of the game the crowd

Vic Halom out jumps the Luton defence in the 1973 quarter-final at Roker Park. After the emotion of the Manchester City clash in the previous round the Luton match was almost an anti-climax. Everybody expected Sunderland to sweep them aside and progress to the semi.

would not go home and kept shouting for Stokoe to come out. Bob Stokoe said that for him it was one of the best moments of the Cup run. There was a policeman who said that he was pleased that we had beat the cockneys. I thought they were supposed to be impartial.

Dave Harrison

Don't Bet On It

A TV programme the night before the Final had Jackie Charlton on it. He said Leeds were going to win with a record score for an FA Cup Final.

George Hoare

Red, White & Curry

We couldn't get a ticket for the Final in 1973 but we still travelled to Wembley. I was with my wife's brother and a friend from Doxford's. We thought we would be able to get a ticket from the touts outside the stadium. We got the overnight coach on the Friday night and before we set off the three of us went to the Boilermakers' Club on the Barbary Coast. The atmosphere was great with everyone in good spirits and convinced we were going to win the Cup. Everyone was wearing red and white. We had a few drinks, then went for a curry and got on the late night coach from Park Lane. I quickly fell asleep on the coach. I think I must of had a bit too much to drink because I woke up the next morning in London with a

adache and curry all down my shirt.
hen we got to Wembley we couldn't
t a ticket for love nor money, they
ere like gold. We needed to find
mewhere to watch the game so I
oned my dad because I knew he had
lations in London. So he phoned
em and they invited us over to their
use. They lived across London and we
arted to panic as the kick-off got closer
d we couldn't find their house. We
t there about half an hour before the
me started. I had never met them
fore but they made us welcome. I felt
ruffy because I had been out all day
d had curry stains on my clothes.
hey only had a black and white telly. I
uld have stayed at home and watched
in colour. When we got back to the
orth East the next day my wife said it
d been brilliant in Sunderland. I wish
hadn't gone to Wembley and just
ayed at home.

lf Henderson

Club Celebrations

When the game was finished
everyone who had been watching
the game on television ran into the
streets to celebrate. The celebrations
continued for the rest of the night. We
went to Gilley Law Club and I have
never known such a great atmosphere.
People were dancing on the tables. The
club was so packed there were three or
four people trying to sit on one chair. I
know a lot of people who were at the
Final said they had wished they could
have been in Sunderland to enjoy the
celebrations.

Audrey Henderson

e greatest save in Sunderland history. Jimmy Montgomery parries Peter Lorimer's goalbound shot on
the bar and to safety.

101

They Gave Everything

I'll never forget the 1973 Cup Final. I don't think there has ever been a Final like it. For a Second Division side those lads were absolutely tremendous. They gave their all. When the final whistle went the Sunderland players flopped on to the turf because the couldn't give any more.

George Forster

Painting the Town Red

All the shops in Easington Lane were decorated in Sunderland colours. The cake shop even had red and white cakes. Everyone was caught up in the atmosphere. It was the impossible dream come true.

Jack Sanderson

Friendly Tykes

There were some great celebrations in London after the game. We mixed with the Leeds fans and there was no trouble.

Alf Henderson

Happy Jonah

For a few bob we used to play guess the score before each game. At every round in the Cup run in 1973 I said Sunderland would get beat. Of course I was glad I lost every time.

George Forster

The Heroes Return

When they came back with the Cup we went to Durham Road by the Double Maxim pub to cheer the bus on its way to Roker Park. You couldn't move the streets were so packed. I had my son Neil with me. He was only five and was dressed up in red and white.

Audrey Henderson

Early Memories

I was too young to remember the 1973 Cup Final but I think I can remember the excitement in Sunderland at the time. Even though I was a young lad I knew something exciting was going on. I do remember being taken to Roker Park by my aunt and uncle when the team brought the Cup back to Sunderland. We had to wait ages for th team to arrive. The streets through the town were so packed their coach had trouble getting to the ground.

Ronnie McGuire

Working for the Milk Cup

I worked overtime on the Saturday to pay for the Milk Cup Final on the Sunday. Coming back we got the 1 o'clock sleeper on the Sunday night from King's Cross. I was back to work a 7.30 on the Monday morning and

orked till 8 o'clock that night. We had
good weekend and the only thing that
oilt it was the game.

ave Harrison

lack Cats Amongst the Canaries

stood in the Norwich End for the
Milk Cup Final in 1985. I was
rrounded by their fans and kept quiet
first. Then another Sunderland
pporter spotted me and stood beside
e. When we were awarded the penalty
e started to hug each other in
elebration. I've often embraced total
rangers at football matches.

ariq Ahmed

Tearful Ending

When Clive Walker missed the
penalty in the Milk Cup Final a
girl near to me started to cry. The man
next to her said, 'Don't worry. We'll get
a goal.' Of course we didn't and that girl
wasn't the only one crying that day.

Billy Swan

Crucial Miss

If Clive Walker had scored that
penalty Sunderland would have won
that game because the crowd would
have won it for them.

Dave Harrison

he Sunderland End at Wembley for the 1985 Milk Cup Final – They had little to cheer about.

Well Beat

We were among the thousands of supporters who made the trip to see the Play-off Final at Wembley in 1990. Before the match we were drinking in a pub in the centre of London. There were half a dozen Swindon supporters sitting at the table next to us. In contrast to our party who were drinking as if the bar might run out of beer, the Swindon supporters did not drink but were happy with their packets of crisps and pop. They reminded me of the Norwich supporters at the 1985 Milk Cup Final. The problem was the same thing happened and these country yokels beat us – the big club with the massive support. The 1-0 scoreline didn't reflect the fact that Swindon dominated the game. In hindsight I think it was important that the defeat wasn't heavier. The FA might have found it more difficult to give Sunderland the promotion spot, after Swindon were found guilty of irregular payments, had the score been something like the 8-0 it could have been.

Jackie Turnbull

Anyone for a Malteser?

It absolutely chucked it down with rain the day of the 1992 Cup Final. Me and my mate James went down to London early to soak up the atmosphere. All we probably soaked up

The Sunderland and Swindon team at Wembley for the 1990 Play-off Final. Sunderland could not repeat the brilliant display that swept aside Newcastle United in the semi-final.

Before the kick-off of the 1992 Cup Final Sunderland supporters make themselves seen and heard.

as half the rain in southern England. I remember taking my place in the stand just before 2.30 p.m. with my red and white shirt sticking to my back. But we didn't care. We were just glad to be here. Getting tickets had been a nightmare. I had written to over ten clubs in the south, virtually begging for any spare tickets. I had even phoned Cambridge United and was put through to their manager John Beck. But he was no help either. Eventually my mate got tickets 48 hours before kick-off, from someone he knew at Aston Villa. He rang me at home that night, after midnight, to say he had them. The game, like the climate, was a washout. I couldn't believe we would lose. Before the match, all the papers said Liverpool would win easily. The whole country thought Liverpool would win the Cup, unless you were from Sunderland. Everyone in Sunderland 'knew' we would win. But when we didn't I nearly cried. After the final whistle I didn't

even stick around to see The Lads get their losers' medals. I just didn't have the heart. The most memorable thing about the day wasn't the game, though. It was the fact that behind me were sitting Gordon Strachan and Rod Stewart. Before the kick-off, people were passing them bits of paper and programmes to sign. I didn't bother. I would have done if Gary Rowell had been sitting behind me, but not Strachan and Stewart. I did offer Rod Stewart a Malteser. He said 'No, thanks', and I added that it was probably just as well as they had been in my pocket all day and were a bit soft.

Neil Henderson

Not the End of the World

Coming away from Wembley in 1992 there was a lot of miserable people.

105

Sunderland supporters settle down for a night outside Roker Park in 1992. Their long vigil was rewarded with tickets for the FA Cup semi-final at Hillsbrough.

A lady is well wrapped up for the long wait for semi-final tickets in 1992.

ut I thought why be miserable about
ne result. There are 90 clubs in the
ootball League who would swap places
ith you right now. Enjoy the day and if
ou win it's great, but if you don't, just
njoy the occasion that is the FA Cup
inal. I didn't expect to win anyway.

ave Harrison

Iopeless View

The seats we had for the Cup Final
were terrible. Wembley wasn't
esigned to be an all-seater stadium.
hey have just put seats on what used
o be terraces and you can hardly see
ne pitch if you are down at ground
vel. Everyone stands up for most of
ne time anyway. Wembley is an awful
round for watching football. No
onder most people stand up.

esley Harrison

All or Nothing

had gone to all the games in the Cup
run with three friends. We went to
ne semi-final at Hillsborough and after
underland won we all said we had to
o to the Final together. It wouldn't
ave been the same if only one of us
ent. Of course it was almost impossible
o get tickets and we never thought we
ould be able to get four. When
underland gave out vouchers at one
natch we all collected the same
umber. If our number was drawn we
ould all go together. If it wasn't we
would all stay at home. Our voucher
wasn't drawn and we all watched the
game on television.

Billy Swan

Meanwhile Back in Sunderland

I was working in a shop in Hylton
Castle at the time of the 1992 Cup
Final and all the customers got into the
spirit of the day. The shop was packed
on the morning of the Final as everyone
wanted to get home to watch the game.
Everyone seemed to be dressed in red
and white. We were wearing rosettes
and the shop was decorated in
Sunderland's colours. You could tell that
some of the people who were willing the
team on had probably never been to a
game in their lives but now they could
talk about nothing else. Everyone was
convinced we were going to win.

Ronnie McGuire

Twice a Loser

At the start of the 1992 Cup run I
put a bet on before the first game. I
put £1 on at 200-1 for Sunderland to
win the Cup. Of course I never dreamt
that we would go all the way to
Wembley. I should have put the bet on
each-way then I would have got £100
when Sunderland reached the Final. But
as Sunderland lost I got nothing.

Alf Henderson

Presto's store in Hylton Castle on Cup Final Day in 1992. Serving behind the counter Mary Ramsay was one of those who was caught up in Cup fever.

Shep the dog shows who he supports on Cup Final Day, 1992.

CHAPTER 7

Around the World

Not all followers of Roker Park football are able to watch the games from the terraces. In many far corners of the world, Sunderland exiles rely on the football edition of the Sunderland Echo for reports and club news. In the past few days reminders for the next season have been sent to nearly 1,000 postal subscribers of whom about one in five are living or working abroad in countries as far apart as Alaska and Afghanistan. Our Afghanistan subscriber – when last heard from – was located in the United States Embassy in Kabul.

Onlooker, *Sunderland Echo*, 19 July 1966.

The Australian Connection – Left to right: Lee Smith, John Hoban and David Hoban.

Sunderland's famous Dutch supporter Hans de Roon outside the Roker End. Hans said if he won the National Lottery he would have bought Roker Park and preserved it exactly as it was.

The Dutchman

I first saw Sunderland play in Holland in the 1950s. They played Sparta Rotterdam and I started to follow them. From the 1960s I would listen to BBC Radio to find out Sunderland scores. It was after the 1973 Cup Final that I started to take more interest and I began subscribing to the *Football Echo*. I was so impressed that a Second Division club had won the famous trophy. In the 1960s I started travelling to Britain to watch games. Most of the matches I saw were in London and it was not until 1980 that I first came to Roker. Sunderland were playing Ipswich who had the two Dutchmen, Muhren and Thijssen in their side. Ipswich won 2-0. When I arrived in Sunderland I was immediately impressed by the seafront. It's not the Bahamas or Benidorm but it is my favourite place. I now live on the seafront very near to Roker Park. The last match at Roker was the 99th game I had seen in Britain. Sunderland had conceded 99 goals and Roker Park was in its 99th year.

Hans de Roon

Down Under

I was born in Australia and since I was thirteen I have supported Sunderland. When I was at school one of my friends started to support Manchester City. I saw Sunderland play on ABC television and I liked their style so I started to follow them. This was in the late 1960s and I have been loyal ever since. I listen for the results every Sunday night. They also show highlights of the English League on a Monday. It is mainly Premiership sides so anyone following teams in the lower leagues misses out. We sometimes watch games live at Rugby League clubs. In 1996 I watched Sunderland play Manchester United in the FA Cup in one of these clubs. We staggered out of the place about 4 o'clock in the morning.

John Hoban

796 (91st YEAR)   SUNDERLAND ECHO AND SHIPPING GAZETTE, SATURDAY, APRIL 18, 1964   THREEPENCE

...NDERLAND WIN THE POINTS AND HIT THE PINK!

...tball Echo Flushes With Success

...ball Echo, which
...white on April 26,
...en for the first
...nderland Football
...l, then to blue at
...of the following
...night resumes its

**...MOTION
...SURED**

of today's matches
...and are assured of
to Division One,
...ablished a lead
...on North End
...ot be overcome
...ne more game to
To mark the
...e Football Echo
again, and pub-
...r-page supplement
...rious season.

traditional pink colour in
celebration of the team's
return to the First Division.

The "Pink 'Un" first turned
white towards the end of the
1912-13 season. The change
was made because supplies
of pink paper could not be
obtained, but the first edition
to be printed on white paper
appeared on the night of
Sunderland's defeat by Aston
Villa in the Cup Final at
Crystal Palace, and it was
commonly said that the
Football Echo had turned
white with shock.

After the first world war the
Football Echo was printed on
blue paper, and there were
repeated requests from
readers that it should return
to its familiar pink. A promise
was made that when Sunderland won the Cup the flush

of victory would be enough
to turn the editions pink.
The day came in 1937, when the
Roker Park club beat Preston
North End at Wembley.
Copies of the Football Echo
were specially printed at
Portsmouth as well as in Sun-
derland for the occasion.
From Portsmouth the edition
was rushed to London where
20,000 copies were sold. The
"Pink 'Un" was a sign to all
that Sunderland had won the
Cup.

It was a great day for Sunderland—and for the Football
Echo, which remained pink
until April 26, 1958 when,
once again it turned white
with shock. When it became
blue at the start of the
following season we gave an
undertaking that it would
not resume its familiar pink
colour until Sunderland
returned to Division I—or
won the F.A. Cup.

Now that day has arrived with
another "Victory Pink 'Un"
to mark the club's promotion.

Charlton's Wakeham Was The Man Of The Match

SUNDERLAND - - - 2   CHARLTON ATHLETIC 1

SUNDERLAND received a great reception from a 50,000 crowd
when they turned out for their final home game of the
season against Charlton Athletic at Roker Park this afternoon.
It was a welcome for the team — and a welcome back to First
Division football, which was virtually
assured by last week's draw with
Southampton.

As there were no fitness problems, Sunderland were
able to rely on an unchanged side, but Charlton changed
the formation of their inside trio to bring Firmani back
at centre forward.

Matthews, who has been standing in for him, switched
to inside right and Peacock displaced Durandt at inside...

...w The Teams Fared Today

...SION I	DIVISION II	DIVISION III
...1 Leicester C. 3	Bury ...... 2 Preston NE 1	Barnsley ... 1 Mansfield .. 1

The *Football Echo* – One of Sunderland's great exports. This edition signalled the return to traditional
pink to celebrate Sunderland's return to the top flight. In the dark days of Second Division football it was
printed on blue/green paper.

Keeping in Touch Long Distance

For many years my mam would send
me occasional copies of the *Echo* and
every copy of the *Pink 'Un* to New
Zealand. I now keep up with news of
Sunderland through the Internet.

Arthur Curtis

Footy Echo to Oz

I subscribe to the *Football Echo*. It
arrives in Australia about a week after
Sunderland's game.

John Hoban

World Service

In 1990 the ship I was working on went into dry dock in Gdansk, Poland. The problem was how to keep in touch with The Lads progress in Division One. I solved this problem by getting the key to the radio room off the 'Marconi' – the radio operator. One Saturday afternoon I was listening to a second half commentary when the Greek captain walked in. 'Hey … Mike … What are you doing in here?' he asked in his broken English. When I told him I was waiting for Sunderland's result he said okay and left me alone.

Michael Stephenson

The Return of Hesford

I hardly missed a Sunderland game in years until I moved to Hong Kong. Now following Sunderland or any football is really difficult. One of the few games I have watched in Hong Kong was when England played a 'Select XI' in 1996. There were some unlikely players in the side to face England with the biggest surprise being Iain Hesford. I told everyone around me that England would have no problem scoring against the former Sunderland 'keeper. How wrong I was when I watched Hesford keep out England for almost the whole of the game. Why couldn't he have played like that at Roker?

Andrew Pace

Eusebio v Monty

I was at the game against Benfica at Roker Park in the early '60s. Eusebio was playing but he was not as well known as he was later to become. I remember he had very little back-lift and he was shooting from the half-way line. He had Monty flying all over.

Dennis Martin

The World Comes to Sunderland

I saw the USSR play Chile in the World Cup in 1966. I didn't pay to get in. I think they had opened the gates at half-time. I thought it was unusual and exciting that people from all over the world had come to Sunderland. This was at the time before going abroad for your holidays was common. I sat in the Fulwell End. There were temporary seats put in just for the World Cup. There was one supporter from Chile who was wearing his country's national dress. It was a leather costume with a big leather hat and he was drinking from a leather wine bottle. He looked like an Argentinian Goucho I had read about at school. I can't remember much about the match because I was more interested in the away supporters. There were also some Korean supporters at the game. They were there supporting the Russian team. If the USSR beat Chile the Koreans would go through to the next round. When I got home the game was on television. I thought it was exciting to be part of something that was shown on TV.

Irene Gibson

acking Atmosphere

When the World Cup games were held at Roker Park in 1966 the mosphere was not the same as at underland matches. Perhaps it was the mporary seating installed for the ompetition. Or it might have been ecause The Lads were not involved.

ommy Allen

low Plane from China

We were on holiday in China and we were coming back on a aturday just in time to see Sunderland lay Newcastle. However, there was a roblem with the plane on the way back nd we were delayed for twenty-four ours and we had to miss the derby me. Instead of watching the game at oker Park we spent a day in Istanbul, hich was some compensation for issing the game.

esley Harrison

n the Dark

have watched every Cup Final on television except Sunderland in 1973. was working in Germany at the time nd there was very little coverage. I idn't even know the result until the ext day. I found out the score on the unday morning and it was difficult to elieve they had actually beaten the reat Leeds team.

eter Gibson

Hungary's Florian Albert, in the mid 1960s he was the best centre forward in the world. He was one of the stars who played at Roker Park in 1966.

I Had To Be There

After I had watched the 1973 Cup Final on television in Australia, I made a promise that I would be at Wembley the next time Sunderland got to the Final. I said to myself, I don't care what situation I am in, or how much money I have or where I am living, I must go to the Final. I didn't think I would have to wait nineteen years for it to happen, but I thank God I

The Supporters' Association presentation night at the Roker Park suite in 1997. Left to right: John Hoban (Australia), Mickey Gray (Castletown) and George Forster (Seaham) show the cosmopolitan following Sunderland has.

told David we were going to Wembley. 'Pack your bags, we're leaving in two days', I told him. He couldn't believe it. David was stunned by the atmosphere at Wembley. He hardly said a word all through the game. He just sat there open-mouthed.

John Hoban

Entertaining the Americans

In the Trip To Jerusalem pub, under Nottingham Castle, Benny Wooton sang the *Lambton Worm*. There was silence from the American tourists in the pub, who were enjoying the performance, but it must have sounded like a foreign language to them with lines like, 'Whisht! Lads, haad yor gobs, An' Aall tell ye 'boot the worm.'

Tommy Keegan

Final Resting Place

My brother was such a staunch supporter, he would phone from wherever he was in the world. Whatever time it was he wanted to hear how Sunderland had got on. His ashes were scattered in the Fulwell End.

Arthur Curtis

was still alive to see it. I enjoyed every minute of it, except the result. It took a while to organise a couple of tickets. I phoned people I knew in Sydney, Brisbane and Adelaide and they suggested people I could contact in England who may get me a ticket. I eventually got two tickets, one for myself and another for my fourteen-year-old son David. I hadn't told him what I was planning because I didn't want to disappoint him if I couldn't get the tickets. When I knew I had them I

CHAPTER 8

You'll Never Walk Alone

he club I was most interested in was Sunderland: at Roker Park I would be able to maintain my north-east connections. A move to Sunderland would enable me to go on living among e good folk in Northumberland and Durham – the best people in the world.

n Shackleton, the Clown Prince of Soccer.

nderland supporters outside Selhurst Park for the relegation decider against Wimbledon.

A cartoon from the *Football Echo* in 1950 shows that supporters' worries about points is nothing new.

Don't Worry

Supporting Sunderland isn't easy on the nerves. A friend and I have bought some Chinese Worry Balls to help us through the season. When things are looking bad we try to ease away our frustrations with them.

Billy Swan

Heartbreaker

In the 1949-50 season Sunderland should have won the League Championship. The game that cost them the title was at home to Manchester City near the end of the season. Sunderland had not lost at Roker all season while City had not won away. Typically Sunderland lost and City's goalkeeper Bert Trautman saved a penalty. If they had won that game they would have finished top. I was so disappointed I said I was never

oming back again. And I didn't for
ears. Although it was not just the
disappointment of not winning the
Championship. I had got married and
had a family to bring up so football
wasn't as important to me as it once
was.

Jack Sanderson

Gamesmanship

When Manchester City goalkeeper
Bert Trautman saved the penalty
taken by Stelling the referee decided the
kick had to be retaken. This angered
Trautman so much he grabbed hold of
the ball and kicked it to the back of the
terraces. I think it may have even gone
out of the ground. Then Stelling put the
second penalty in exactly the same
place and Trautman saved again.

George Hoare

Something Lacking

I've seen some very good Sunderland
teams but perhaps the finest was in
the late 1940s and very early '50s. They
were definitely good enough to win the
Championship but just fell short. I feel
that the only reason was that they
weren't pushed hard enough.

Ron Gormley

It Doesn't Rain But It Pours

One of the lowest attendances at
Roker Park was against Cardiff
City in 1953. It was a re-arranged mid-
week match which had to be played at
the end of the season. It was an
absolutely atrocious evening. The rain
had pelted down all day and was still
chucking it down throughout the
match. I was working down Sans Street
at the time, serving my apprenticeship,
and had arranged to meet a friend, who
went to all the matches with me, at our
usual spot in the Roker End. I was
wearing a brand new rain coat but still
got absolutely soaked. At half-time we
decided to pay a bit extra to go in the
Clock Stand. This did not prevent my
rain coat being absolutely ruined and I
got quite an ear-bashing when I got
home. I felt I must be serving an
apprenticeship in idiocy. My main
recollection of the match is Harry
Kirtley being tripped from behind and
going face down in a gigantic puddle.
The poor lad almost drowned.

George Hoare

The Unthinkable

The day Sunderland went to
Portsmouth for the final match of
1957-58 season I went to Roker Park
with my Uncle Arthur to see
Sunderland Reserves play Horden
Colliery Welfare. We stood in the Clock
Stand near the Roker End. This was
before any seats were in the Clock

When Sunderland were relegated for the first time in their history it was not only the *Football Echo* ball that was in tears.

Stand. With a couple of minutes to go my uncle told me to go out of the ground and run round to the players' entrance to see if I could find out how the first team were doing. They had to win to have any chance of staying in Division One. I duly obliged and ran as fast as I could. I asked everyone I came to and eventually found out that The Lads were 2-0 up. Overjoyed I raced back to my uncle and gasped out the great news. A few seconds later the final whistle went on the pitch and the tannoy then announced the score but added that Leicester had won 1-0 at Birmingham and therefore Sunderland were relegated for the first time ever. We both trudged home with not a word spoken between us. I can remember crying and I'm certain that Uncle Arthur was fighting back the tears.

Phil Curtis

Culture Shock

In the 1950s I would go to the match with a friend of mine who lived in Darlington. We would go to nearly all of Sunderland's home games and occasionally we would watch Middlesbrough play. They were in the Second Division at the time. We thought the Second Division was rubbish compared to the First and I thought if Sunderland get relegated I don't want to watch football like this. But you never thought Sunderland would go down. They had always played in the First Division and that is what we were used to. The relegation season in 1957-58 was a very bad spell for Sunderland and there was a lot of animosity towards the manager Alan Brown. He hadn't been at Sunderland for very long and he seemed to be the person most fans blamed. He didn't have very much money to spend but buying players wasn't his style, he preferred to develop young players. Some of his ideas about improving the youth system and training facilities changed the whole nature of the club.

George Hoare

Sad Victory at Liverpool

I was first taken regularly to Roker Park by my Uncle Arthur during the 1956-57 season. He had bought two season tickets for the Main Stand. The following season we began to go to St James' on alternate weeks and stood in the East Stand. We always went with our neighbour, Jimmy Fenton, who was a Sunderland fan. I was twelve in 1961 when Sunderland were drawn away to Liverpool in the FA Cup and arrangements were made for Uncle Arthur, myself, Jimmy Fenton and one of his mates to go down to Liverpool for the game. For some reason during the week of the match my uncle found he couldn't go and that in turn meant that I also couldn't go without him. Jimmy, however, did go. In Manchester the car he was in broke down but he managed to hitch a lift home in a coach from Steels Engineering Works. On the way back, near Northallerton, the coach skidded on black ice and went off the road. The passengers got off the bus and some of them began to push the coach back on to the road. No sooner had they begun when another coach skidded on the same place and careered into the back of the first coach, killing four and injuring fifteen people. Jimmy was one of the lads who were killed. I recall a knock on our front door in Dock Street very late that night. It was the police. They were looking for Jimmy's address. My Uncle Arthur took them to break the news to Jimmy's mother. Next morning he travelled to Northallerton

Michael Bridges and Phil Curtis. Michael is a Tynesider playing for Sunderland while Sunderland-born Phil was once on Newcastle United's books. Michael is a brilliant prospect having scored some crucial goals for Sunderland and has represented Young England. Phil's playing career was ended when he broke his leg playing for Newcastle's Youth team.

to identify the body. Jimmy was twenty-seven and the other lads who died were all teenagers.

Phil Curtis

Hylton Castle Lad

Michael Oxberry was one of the supporters killed that night coming back from Liverpool. Michael was a goalkeeper for Hylton Castle and the YOC Minor League donated a trophy to his name.

Mickey Bute

Reading Tragedy

After Sunderland won at Reading in the 1973 Cup run two supporters died in a car crash on the journey home. One of the them was a workmate, Kevin Bottoms from Boldon. He was nineteen and the other lad was only sixteen. Bob Stokoe and the Sunderland players were at his funeral.

Terry McIvor

Last Farewell

In November 1988 three Sunderland supporters were killed in a car crash on their way to the match at Oxford. They were all in their early twenties. In Monroes (formerly the Boilermakers' Club) before Sunderland's next home game a collection was taken for their families. As the collection trays were going round a deafening chorus of Ha' Way The Lads went up. Hundreds of Sunderland supporters were paying a final tribute to three of their own.

Mark Taylor

Chelsea at Roker & Seaburn

Sunderland needed one point against Chelsea in the final game of the 1962-63 season to secure promotion to the First Division. The night before the game I went to the Seaburn Hotel with a few friends to have a look at the

Chelsea team who were staying there. We were only kids and were in awe of these well known players. Their goalkeeper, Peter Bonetti was looking out to sea. I wondered what he thought of our seafront? It seemed strange to be so close to them at Seaburn and the following day see them play against our heroes at Roker Park.

There was a big crush to get into the game and I was separated from my friends. I was only twelve and there were much bigger lads around me and I was crushed against the wall. I was near to the point of passing out when a policeman pulled me clear. I got into the ground but still felt dizzy. The game was really disappointing with Sunderland beaten 1-0. I couldn't believe Sunderland had failed to win promotion. Chelsea went up instead. After they beat us they needed to win against Portsmouth a few days later to be promoted. Chelsea won 7-0. I was so disappointed at the end of the Chelsea game that I couldn't face going home. I walked around the town centre then trudged home to Southwick.

Peter Gibson

Disappointment in Wales

The lasting memory of Sunderland's match at Wrexham on the last day of the 1978-79 season was the huge following we had. Parked outside the Racecourse Ground was the longest line of coaches I've ever seen. Over ten thousand Sunderland supporters packed a stand running the length of the pitch as well as a section behind the goal, which was full to bursting point. The game itself was end to end stuff with the blistering pace of Alan Brown and the goalkeeping heroics of Barry Siddall helping Sunderland to a 2-1 win which supporters thought would give us promotion. There were thousands of fans on the pitch celebrating and then the news came through that Brighton and Stoke had won so they would go up instead. I was talking to a friend recently and he revealed he was also at the match. He was a teenager at the time and the disappointment hit him hard. When he got back to his coach he said to his mate, 'Bloody hell. I can't believe we are not going up.' The travel club steward turned to him and said sharply, 'Hey, hey, hey … cut that out or you'll be off the coach. It's only a game!' For some it is.

Jackie Turnbull

The Lowest of the Low

When Laurie McMenemy became manager there seemed to be a wave of optimism that swept over Sunderland. It seemed at last we had a 'big name' manager to lead us to success. Even when the team had a poor start to the season the fans never lost belief. Even the Full Members Cup was well supported. For the game against Grimsby there was over 10,000 at Roker. The prices were lowered and me and my friends went into the seats for the first time. It was an exciting game which Sunderland won in a penalty shoot-out. That was a rare highlight in a depressing couple of seasons. I think the

lowest I have ever felt as a Sunderland supporter was relegation to the Third Division.

Billy Swan

New Horizons

When Sunderland were relegated to the Third Division I was disappointed but it did give me the opportunity to visit some grounds I had never been to. I only missed two games and both of those were mid-week. By the end of the year I had put 28,000 miles on my car and most of that was through travelling to away matches.

Dave Harrison

Manchester Blues

The game at Manchester City in May 1991 was yet another last day of the season dog fight. The day didn't start too promisingly as the car we were travelling in got a flat tyre on the M62. By the time we reached Manchester the streets surrounding Maine Road were deserted. As we parked up and quickly made our way to the turnstiles a roar went up. We later discovered Niall Quinn had given City the lead. There were further delays when we were sent from one gate to another, hundreds of yards apart, before getting into the ground at the first gate we had gone to. We were in at last, only twenty minutes late. Sunderland were on the attack, there was a scramble in the goalmouth

121

Part of the mass ranks of Sunderland supporters at Maine Road in 1991. The travelling army left disappointed as Sunderland were yet again relegated.

and Gary Bennett forced the ball home. The atmosphere was by now electric. John Kay got to the by line and sent over an inch perfect cross for Marco Gabbiadini to head Sunderland in front. But Man City spoilt the party by first equalising and then scoring the winner. That result sent us down and we were out of the top flight for five seasons. Before leaving Maine Road the Sunderland supporters gave an amazing display of loyalty by staying behind after the final whistle to salute Denis Smith and his team. For more than half an hour *You'll Never Walk Alone* and *We'll Keep The Red Flag Flying High* echoed around the three quarter empty stadium. More than 15,000 Sunderland supporters would not leave until the manager and his men came out of the dressing room. And when they did they

were given an emotional reception. You could see that it clearly affected Denis Smith deeply and perhaps it swayed him to stay at Roker rather than leave for Stoke City. He had been linked with the manager's job there and in hindsight it probably would have been better for him and the club if he had left then. He could have gone to his beloved Victoria Ground and Sunderland could have made a fresh start.

Jackie Turnbull

Who is the Home Team?

The most moving scenes I've ever seen before a match were down at Selhurst Park for the last match in the

122

remiership against Wimbledon. Thousands travelled down and from a distance it must have looked like the streets were paved with red and white. Me and my two mates just stood outside the ground in awe, as coach after coach came in. There were coaches, minibuses and cars all with red and white scarves and flags. Loads of kids had their faces painted and everyone was full of optimism that we would win, and stay up. All the pubs around the ground were closed or full. I asked a copper where we could get a drink and he said our best bet was to get a can from the off-licence and enjoy the sunshine. So we stood there on the pavement, drink in hand, and sung our hearts out.

On the way into the ground we saw Gary Bennett. He looked dead cool in a long coat and was getting a tremendous reception from the Sunderland fans. My mate, Tony, a Chelsea fan along for the ride, was dead impressed that Gary Bennett had come to support The Lads. Inside the ground things were just as impressive as out in the streets. There was red and white absolutely everywhere. It might have been an away game, but we 'took' the stadium that day. When the players came out they seemed almost embarrassed by it all. A funny thing about that day was that the team played in white. I think it would have been nice to play in red and white. Since Wimbledon play in blue, there would have been no colour clash. I just think that playing in red and white in front of a red and white army would have been the best way to end the season. But never mind.

Another funny thing was that we played terrible, considering the importance of the game. All we needed

Former Sunderland favourite Gary Bennett lends support for the vital last game of the season at Wimbledon.

Supporters stay behind after the final whistle to await the result of the Spurs-Coventry game. The Sky Blues surprise victory at White Hart Lane meant Sunderland's stay in the top flight was all too brief.

was a win and we would stay in the Premiership. But the players didn't seem to ever look like scoring. It was unbelievable. When Wimbledon scored the inevitable winning goal the Sunderland fans reacted by singing even louder than before. It was amazing and sad at the same time. When the final whistle went, the players all ran straight off. All except for Craig Russell. As he trudged slowly off the pitch, we sang a chorus of *Walking in a Russell Wonderland*, and at the tunnel he stopped and bowed down to us in humble appreciation. I had a lump in my throat. Meanwhile up the road, Spurs and Coventry were still playing. They had kicked-off fifteen minutes later than us. Everyone waited on the terraces for that result to come in. Anything other than a Coventry win and we wouldn't be relegated. I couldn't

stand the tension. Me and my mates left for the station and it was on the platform that he heard the news. It confirmed what we already knew in our hearts. Another wasted year.

Neil Henderson

The World Turned Upside Down

Defeat against Wimbledon give me my first taste of relegation. Sunderland have always been classed as a team who go up one season and down the next and when this happens you realise how great winning the League is and how bad being relegated is. We went into the last game of the season knowing if we won we were up. But Wimbledon were the team we needed to

utside the Railway Telegraph, Thornton Heath, the 'quiet' London pub recommended to travelling fans
the London branch SAFC Supporters Association.

:at. The Red Army were on the march
ith 15,000 Sunderland fans going to
:lhurst Park to see The Lads and many
ore going down to try and get a ticket
.ere.

On the way to London everybody was
ɔpeful with one man even saying 'I'll
ıt my house on a Sunderland win
ɔday.' It's a good job he didn't. Just
:fore 4 o'clock The Lads took to the
:ld and they were greeted by a loud
ɔar which really, because of the way
ıey played, they didn't deserve. By
ılf-time we hadn't had a shot at goal

and I feared the worst. In the second
half we were just as bad and I will have
nightmares about a Paul Stewart miss
when he seemed he must score but
didn't. Then came the moment when
the Dons scored and my whole world
turned upside down. The game ended
1-0 and that's when my flood of tears
began.

I couldn't believe it but there was still
a glimmer of hope. Spurs v Coventry
had kicked off 15 minutes late.
Coventry were leading 2-1 but if Spurs
could score we would stay up. Many

stayed at Selhurst Park to cheer Spurs on and choruses of *Come On You Spurs* were heard but they amounted to nothing. Coventry held on and we were down. I had the worst feeling I had ever felt as far as football was concerned in the bottom of my stomach. Then the song *Always Look On The Bright Side Of Life* was heard but to me there wasn't a bright side, we were down.

Andrea Lane

The Crying Game

I was crying when I heard the result at Selhurst Park. Just like I was crying when we were relegated to the Third Division or when Holland were beaten in the World Cup.

Hans de Roon

Stadium of Tears

I've cried so many times while supporting Sunderland. I've cried when we have been relegated and I've cried when we lost at Wembley. I have even cried with joy … sometimes.

Ronnie McGuire

The Greatest

We may not have always watched the best football in the world at Roker Park but we have the best

supporters in the land. Who else would put up with all the disappointments we have had over the years. The fans at Sunderland will always be Premiership class, even if the team isn't.

Billy Swan

Forever Sunderland

The funeral of Sunderland supporter Billy Bainbridge (known affectionately as Billy Buttons) brought home just how passionate he felt about the club. As we entered the chapel instead of a hymn being played *Cheer Up Peter Reid* greeted mourners. The service finished with *You'll Never Walk Alone*.

Mark Taylor

Billy Bainbridge known to thousands Sunderland supporters as Billy Buttons.

The Sale of the Century – Supporters got their chance to buy their own piece of Roker Park at the auction June 1997.

The end of almost a century of football memories – The Clock Stand and Fulwell End in the progress of demolition in August 1997.

Glossary

Below is a list of some of the local terms and expressions used in the book which may sound unfamiliar to some. Also included are places, such as pubs, clubs, schools and factories, which are mentioned in the text – many of which have now gone. For those readers who don't remember pre-decimalisation, there is a guide to some of the old prices.

Bairns - Children. Not a slang word but a derivation of an Old English word 'bearns' which has survived in the North East to the present day.

Bait - Sandwiches, etc, taken to work, school or match.

Barbary Coast - An old name for part of Monkwearmouth.

Cadged - Begged, borrowed.

Canny - Good, clever, skilful, artful, wily, shrewd and supernaturally wise.

Cat and Dog Steps - A popular sun bathing spot at Roker.

Chin - Punch on the jaw.

Fish Lot - Fish and chips.

Gadgy - Man.

Gannin - Going.

Glasgow Handshake - Head-butt.

Ha'Way The Lads - Sunderland's famous rallying cry.

Mackies Corner - The junction of Fawcett Street and High Street West.

Pattie Lot - Portion of chips with a fish cake or savoury slice.

Saveloy Dips - Seasoned sausage in a 'dipped' bun, usually with pea's pudding and sage and onion stuffing.

Shanks' Pony - Travelling by foot.

Suddick - Old name for Southwick.

Clubs and Nightclubs - The Boilermakers', Boldon, Downhill, Farringdon, Gilley Law, Hylton Castle, La Strada.

Cinemas, Theatres and Leisure - Cora, Crowtree Leisure Centre, Empire, Exce Bowling, Havelock, King's, The Rink.

Factories and Shops - Buchan and Lowings, Davey Browns, HMV, Inkerman Print, Jacky White's Market, Joplings, Prestos (Hylton Castle), Redhead & Browns, Steels.

Pubs - The Blandford, The Cambridge The Divan, Double Maxim, Hendon Hotel, Park Inn, Queen's Hotel, Red Lion, Round Robin, The Salutation, The Wolseley.

Schools - British Day School, Diamond Hall, Hendon Board, Redby, St Hilda's Southmoor, Stansfield Street, Thornhi

Shipyards - Doxford's, Greenwell's, Thompson's.

Pre-Decimalisation Prices
3d, threepenny bit - 1p approx.
6d, tanner, sixpence - $2\frac{1}{2}$p,
1/-, shilling, bob - 5p,
1/6 - $7\frac{1}{2}$p
Half a crown - $12\frac{1}{2}$p
7/6 - $37\frac{1}{2}$p
9/- - 45p
Thirty bob - £1.50

1 lb = 500g